Debbie Eason

ESSENTIALS

GCSE Design & Technology
Graphic Products
Revision Guide

Contents

Contents

Communication Techniques

Sketching

Freehand sketching is a **quick method** that can be used to create design ideas and accentuate **shape and form**. Freehand means that no straight edges are used. You can use pens or pencils, e.g. H (hard), HB (general purpose) and B (black, soft).

Crating is where you draw a **3D box** around the whole object to help break it down into a shape. This method enables you to draw in three dimensions (3D). You can use a ruler to help you draw straight lines.

N.B. You should always annotate your sketches against the design specification.

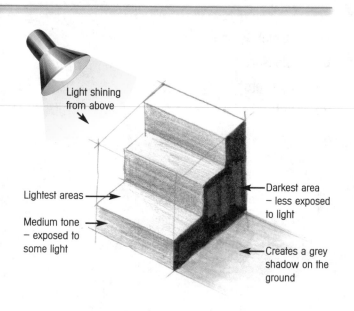

Crating

Construction lines (form a crate)

Working plane (or side panel)

Hidden lines

Rendering, Tone and Texture

Rendering means applying **colour** and **shade** to an object to make it look realistic.

You can create **tone** by using shading to show areas of **light** and **shadow**. Don't forget to show where your light source is coming from.

You can add **texture** to a sketch or drawing by using pencil or pen marks to create the illusion of a **surface effect**.

These techniques can be used to illustrate different materials, for example wood, concrete, metal, plastic, glass and textiles.

Light shining from above

Lightest areas

Medium tone – exposed to some light

Darkest area – less exposed to light

Creates a grey shadow on the ground

Tools

You can use the following tools on their own or together to create different effects:
- **Marker pens** – quick and effective.
- **Pastels** – good for creating tone; can be messy if you don't 'fix' your drawing.
- **Coloured pencils** – inexpensive and commonly used; can be used with marker pens.
- **Paints** – time consuming and can be messy, but watercolours make good backgrounds.

Primary and Secondary Colours   AQA • OCR

The three **primary colours** are red, yellow and blue. They can't be created by mixing colours together.

Secondary colours, e.g. green, purple and orange, are produced when two primary colours are mixed.

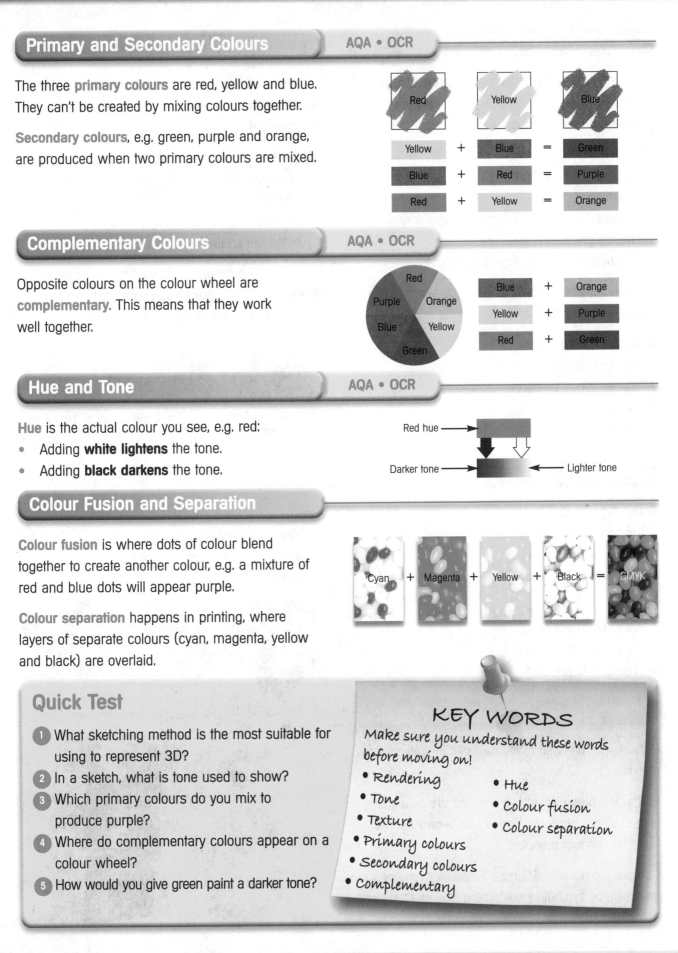

Yellow	+	Blue	=	Green
Blue	+	Red	=	Purple
Red	+	Yellow	=	Orange

Complementary Colours   AQA • OCR

Opposite colours on the colour wheel are **complementary**. This means that they work well together.

Blue	+	Orange
Yellow	+	Purple
Red	+	Green

Hue and Tone   AQA • OCR

Hue is the actual colour you see, e.g. red:
- Adding **white lightens** the tone.
- Adding **black darkens** the tone.

Red hue →

Darker tone → ← Lighter tone

Colour Fusion and Separation

Colour fusion is where dots of colour blend together to create another colour, e.g. a mixture of red and blue dots will appear purple.

Colour separation happens in printing, where layers of separate colours (cyan, magenta, yellow and black) are overlaid.

Cyan + Magenta + Yellow + Black = CMYK

Quick Test

1. What sketching method is the most suitable for using to represent 3D?
2. In a sketch, what is tone used to show?
3. Which primary colours do you mix to produce purple?
4. Where do complementary colours appear on a colour wheel?
5. How would you give green paint a darker tone?

KEY WORDS

Make sure you understand these words before moving on!
- Rendering
- Tone
- Texture
- Primary colours
- Secondary colours
- Complementary
- Hue
- Colour fusion
- Colour separation

Colour

Language and Meaning

Colours are **associated** with different meanings. Knowing the different meanings can help you when making design decisions.

Blue is...
- a natural colour from the sky
- calming
- used for all sorts of purposes, e.g. packaging / road signs
- associated with intelligence and unity.

In many religious beliefs, blue brings peace and keeps the bad spirits away.

Red is associated with...
- flushed cheeks
- raised blood pressure
- anger
- danger.

In China, red represents happiness and prosperity, but in other countries, it can represent mourning or communism.

Yellow is associated with...
- sunshine
- happiness / joy
- warmth
- being cheerful.

But it can also represent cowardice or deceit. In different countries yellow can represent mourning, courage and peace or signify the dead.

Other Colours

Green represents...
- growth / renewal / the environment
- envy
- balance / harmony.

Orange...
- is vibrant / warm
- is a citrus fruit colour
- represents good health.

Purple...
- represents royalty / nobility
- represents lavender
- can boost creativity.

Image

Colours can be used to indicate certain categories of product.

White and **blue** denote hygiene and are associated with cleaning products. **Green** and **brown** denote healthy / organic products.

Colours are used in different **cultures** or **religions** to represent or symbolise something. You need to be careful not to use colours that can offend anyone.

Logos
AQA • OCR

Logos are symbols that **convey a meaning**:
- They tend to be about a product or a company.
- Some logos are well known enough to be described from memory, e.g. Cadbury.

Cadbury

Trademarks
AQA • OCR

A trademark is a word, phrase, symbol or design (or a combination of these), which identifies and distinguishes the goods of one company. They are usually registered to the company, i.e. legally owned by the company, so no one else can use them.

An **SM mark** is used when a company delivers a service and are waiting for their registration to go through, so they can use the ® '**registered**' symbol.

The **copyright** symbol is put against a company name to prevent other companies from copying their product or service.

Royal Mail

TM	**SM**	**®**	**©**
Trademark	Service mark	Registered	Copyright

Corporate Identity and Brand Names

Corporate Identity...
- is a logo and / or title which represents what a company is all about
- is a company's **visual expression** or 'look'
- can run through all of a company's products.

Brand names...
- are the names of products
- might tell the customer what the product is all about, e.g. Cadbury's 'Crunchie' is also named because of the filling inside the bar.

Quick Test

1. According to some religious beliefs, what does blue represent?
2. Name two things that the colour green represents.
3. Why should you be careful which colours you choose for religious and cultural organisations?
4. What is the main function of a logo?
5. Explain what a trademark is.
6. Explain what a corporate identity is.

KEY WORDS
Make sure you understand these words before moving on!
- Association
- Cultures
- Logos
- Trademark
- Corporate identity
- Brand names

Typography

Typography AQA

Typography is the **art of lettering** which is…
- used to create an **effect**
- used to create a **meaning**
- used to make an **impact** so customers will recognise and buy a product.

This image is a representation of a car wash. The bubbles in the lettering represent the soap suds. The brush and the reflection below have been added as they're associated with washing a car. This shows how you can use strong imagery to highlight the meaning of a word.

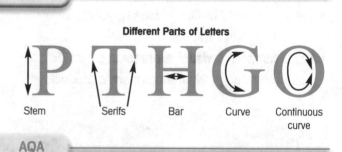

Font

A **font** is…
- a design for a set of characters
- a specific typeface of a certain size and style.

Most word processing programs have a font menu that allows you to choose the typeface, size and style of the text.

Arial	▼	11	▼	**B**	*I*	U
Times New Roman	▼	16	▼	**B**	*I*	U
Courier New	▼	14	▼	**B**	*I*	U
Helvetica Oblique	▼	6	▼	**B**	*I*	U

Parts of Letters AQA

Lettering styles come in…
- **capital letters** – also known as 'upper case'
- **small letters** – also known as 'lower case'.

Letters are made up of different parts.

Different Parts of Letters

| Stem | Serifs | Bar | Curve | Continuous curve |

Serifs AQA

Serifs are **strokes** which finish off the end of the stems.

Sans serifs are letters **without extra strokes** on the ends.

There are different styles of serif fonts, for example…
- full bracketed
- hairline
- slab
- slab bracketed.

Serif   Sans serif

| Full bracketed | Hairline | Slab | Slab bracketed |

Letter Spacing

The ease with which text can be read depends on the spaces in between the letters and words. Sometimes the space between individual letters needs altering so the word looks more **evenly spaced**. There are two types of adjustments.

Kerning is where the spacing between **pairs of letters** is adjusted.

Tracking is where the spacing between **all letters** is adjusted.

Kerning

AT AV Fo Kd To Vc Wc r, y, 118
Unkerned letters

AT AV Fo Kd To Vc Wc r, y, 118
Kerned letters

Tracking

Tracking reduces letter space in 12pt Times
No tracking

Tracking reduces letter space in 12pt Times
Tracked

Text Alignment and Word Spacing

In computing, the following symbols show how you can align text to fit with pictures or margins:

Left Align   Centre Align   Right Align   Justified

Justified text is the **alignment of text** within a column where the text sits flush with the left and right hand margins. This method is used in typesetting and is how you would normally type text. **Newspapers** often **justify** the text to cope with the columns and layout on each page.

Word spacing is the space between words.

The size of a small 'n' is normally used between small letters:

Goodnspacing

The size of a large 'O' is normally used between large lettering:

GOODOSPACING

Quick Test

1. What is a serif style lettering?
2. What is sans serif lettering?
3. Name four types of serif font.
4. What are capital letters also known as?
5. What is typography the 'art' of?
6. Explain what justified text is.

KEY WORDS

Make sure you understand these words before moving on!
- Typeface
- Serif
- Sans serif
- Kerning
- Tracking
- Justified

Drawing Techniques and Materials

Grids and Under-lays

You can use a grid underneath your sheet of paper to help with your designing.

A **square grid**...
- comes in mm/cms and inches
- can be used for measuring letters and scaled plans.

An **isometric (ISO) grid**...
- comes in a variety of size grids and in line or dot format
- can be used to help you get the angles correct for isometric projections.

You can also use grids for perspective drawing. All these grids save time when you are drawing. There are also ICT packages to draw with.

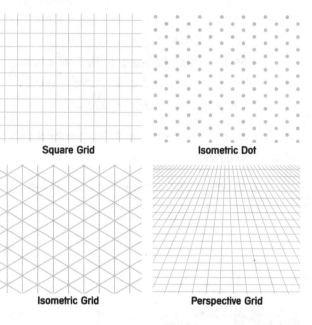

Square Grid   Isometric Dot

Isometric Grid   Perspective Grid

Tracing Paper

An **image** from a magazine or picture can be copied onto tracing paper and then transferred onto any type of paper. **Working drawings** can be done on tracing paper too.

You could even use a grid sheet behind the tracing paper to produce a drawing without a grid on it.

Of course, it's much easier to do any of these processes on a computer by using a drawing package / scanner.

Paper and Board Measurements

It's important to choose the right type of paper and board to achieve the best quality finish.

Papers come in various **weights** and **textures**. For example...
- 100 grams per metre squared (g/m² or gsm) refers to the weight of one square metre
- anything over 200g/m² is classed as board.

Paper comes in many different **sizes**. The most commonly used ones are classified in the 'A' series. They are based on the A0 size, which has an area of 1m². The smaller sizes fit within the A0 size:
- A1 measures 594mm x 841mm (2 x A1 = 1 x A0)
- A2 measures 420mm x 594mm (2 x A2 = 1 x A1)
- A3 measures 297mm x 420mm (2 x A3 = 1 x A2)
- A4 measures 210mm x 297mm (2 x A4 = 1 x A3)
- A5 measures 148mm x 210mm (2 x A5 = 1 x A4)
- A6 measures 105mm x 148mm (2 x A6 = 1 x A5)

Drawing Techniques and Materials

Types of Paper and Board

Type	Description	Uses
Corrugated card	Has two or more layers of card with a fluted inner section to add thickness and strength with very little increase in weight.	Used for packing objects which need protection during transportation.
Cartridge paper / photocopy paper	Good quality surface for pencils, pens and markers. The soft surface can also be used with crayons, pastels, inks, watercolours and gouache.	Used for design drawings, sketching and for good quality marker pen presentations.
White board	This is a strong medium where the surface has been bleached to provide an excellent surface for printing.	Used for good quality packaging and book covers.
Duplex board	This provides a less expensive alternative to white board and also a different texture for printing.	Used mainly in food packaging since recycled material can't be used for this purpose.
Grey board	Provides a reliable, stiff surface.	Used in schools for model-making / book-making.
Bleed-proof paper	Has similar qualities to cartridge paper but is specifically good at isolating water-based paints and pens so they don't run into areas where you don't want them.	Used in **high quality** presentations.
Layout paper (detail paper)	A thin, fairly **transparent** white paper which provides a cheap medium for designers to use for visualising a project or design.	Used in preparation of final ideas to trace images.
Cardboard	A cheap, **recyclable**, stiff board with a good surface to print onto.	Used for packaging, boxes and cartons.

Quick Test

1. What is the main use for corrugated cardboard?
2. What kind of paper is layout paper?
3. What is bleed-proof paper similar to?
4. At which weight does paper become classed as board?
5. What units of measurement does a square grid come in?

KEY WORDS

Make sure you understand these words before moving on!

- Square grid
- Isometric grid (ISO)
- Transferred
- High quality
- Transparent
- Recyclable

Practice Questions

1. What type of grid sheet could you use to draw lettering?

....

2. Write the rest of the word GRID below:

3. Give two reasons why a company should have a corporate identity.

   a) ....

   b) ....

4. What does this symbol mean?

....

5. If you are kerning your letters, what do you do to them?

....

6. a) Name the three colours which can't be made by mixing colours together.

   ....

   b) What are these colours known as?

   ....

7. What are opposite colours on the colour wheel known as?

....

8 What type of products is green associated with?

_____

9 What can this grid sheet specifically be used for?

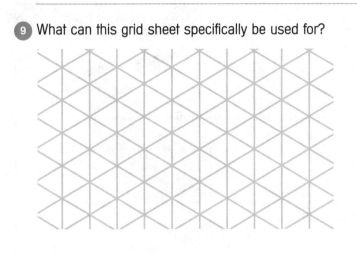

_____

10 Name three ways of changing the appearance of a font, e.g. using bold.

a) _____

b) _____

c) _____

11 What is colour fusion?

_____

12 What are the parts called that the arrows are pointing to?

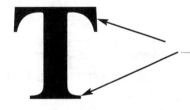

13 Why would you adjust the spacing between letters?

_____

14 Are the following statements **true** or **false**?

a) The copyright symbol means that any company can copy the product or service. _____

b) The size of a small 'n' is normally used between lower case words. _____

c) The colour brown is usually associated with hygiene products. _____

Drawing Tools

Equipment	Description	
Pair of compasses	• Used with a pencil or technical pen • Used to draw accurate circles or arcs • Used for working drawings	
Protractor	• Measures angles • Made from plastic • Either circular or semi-circular	
Ruler	• A 300mm ruler is used for measuring in any part of your design stage	
Scale ruler	• Already has different scales worked out for you so you can draw working drawings and spend less time working out the measurements	
Set square	• Used to draw specific angles for orthographic and isometric drawings • Two main types of set square: one has an angle of 45° and the other 30°/60° • Used with a drawing board	
Drawing board	• A board with a parallel motion to help do working drawings by hand	
Ellipse **template**	• Helps draw ellipses in 3D drawing • Also comes as an isometric ellipse template	
Circle template	• Has different size circles and guides so you know where the centre is • Is easier than using a pair of compasses for small circles	
French curves / flexible curves	• Both help to draw arcs; the 'flexi' curve can be adjusted to any arc you need	Flexible Curve French Curve

Pencils

Graphite pencils, e.g. 2B and HB, are used for shading and toning ideas. 2H and 6H are used for construction lines (like in the 'crating method').

Coloured pencils are used for light shading and toning on your design ideas. They are available in water soluble / pastel or graphite.

Mechanical pencils...
- are also known as 'propelling pencils'
- contain a push mechanism to eject the lead through the tip of the pencil
- are more accurate than normal graphite pencils.

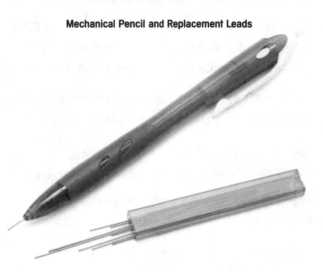

Mechanical Pencil and Replacement Leads

Pens

Fineline black technical pens are...
- used for sketching / outlines
- most commonly used in size 0.5
- useful to have in sizes 0.1, 0.3 and 0.7.

Marker pens are...
- used to cover larger areas with colour
- available in a wide range of colours / tones.

Fibre-tipped pens are...
- used for bold shading and outlining
- water-based / spirit-based
- good for sketching design ideas
- cheaper than fineline technical pens.

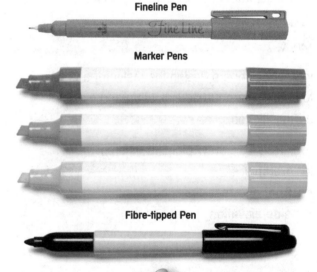

Fineline Pen

Marker Pens

Fibre-tipped Pen

Quick Test

1. What is the main function of a protractor?
2. What does a scale ruler have on it?
3. Which pencils can be used for toning and shading?
4. What are marker pens used for?
5. Fineline technical pens are cheaper than fibre-tipped pens. True or false?

KEY WORDS
Make sure you understand these words before moving on!
- Protractor
- Ellipse
- Graphite pencils
- Mechanical pencils

Plan Drawings

Scale

Scale is written as a mathematical term called **ratio**:
- An object **half** the size of the original is 1:2.
- An object **twice** the size of the original is 2:1.

1:20, **1:25**, **1:50**, **1:100** are the most commonly used scales in architecture and interior design.

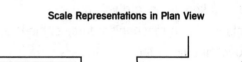

Scale Drawing

2:1   1:2

Scale Representations

Working drawings are produced by designers in industry.

Architects use scale picture representations of household items, in plan view.

Exhibition and interior designers also produce scale drawings, but not as detailed as architects.

Scale Representations in Plan View

Bath   Door   Cooker

Building Drawings

Interior designers design the inside of a building, to show where furniture, lighting and electrics are positioned.

Architects can draw plans in different views, for example…
- **front** and **rear** elevation
- **side elevation**
- **plan view**.

Rear Elevation of a House

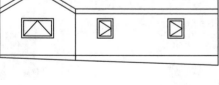
Side Elevation of a House

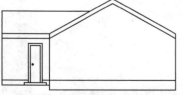

Floor Plan

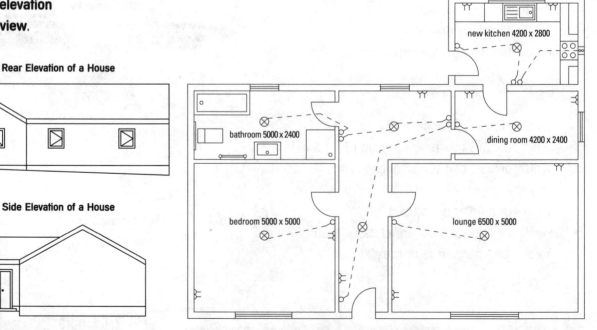

new kitchen 4200 x 2800

bathroom 5000 x 2400

dining room 4200 x 2400

bedroom 5000 x 5000

lounge 6500 x 5000

Planometric Technique

A **planometric** technique gives you a **3D impression** of a product or interior:

- You can draw the plan view to scale, and then tilt it to either 45°/45° or 60°/30°.
- The height needs to be reduced to $\frac{3}{4}$ of the actual size in a 45° planometric, or it will look too tall.

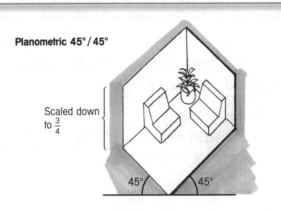

Planometric 45°/45°

Scaled down to $\frac{3}{4}$

45°   45°

Methods of Enlarging

There are various methods of **enlarging images**. A few are as follows:

- **Overhead projector** – photocopy onto transparent film, then project onto the surface you need to draw onto.

- A **photocopier** reduces and enlarges, for example between A4 and A3.
- **Computer software** scans an image and reduces or enlarges, for example between A4 and A3.

Recognising Different Shapes

You need to know what the following shapes are:

- **Triangle** (3 sided), one of the strongest structural shapes.
- **Quadrilateral** (4 sided), for example square, rhombus, rectangle, parallelogram, trapezium and kite.
- **Polygon** (multi-sided), for example pentagon, hexagon and octagon.
- **Ellipse** (inclined circle).

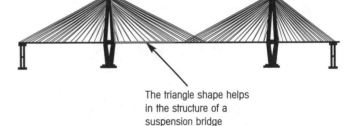

Suspension Bridge

The triangle shape helps in the structure of a suspension bridge

Quick Test

1. Name four different scales that interior designers and architects would use.
2. Give the scale ratio for a drawing, which is half the size of the actual object.
3. What view point does a plan show objects from?
4. What angle is used on a planometric drawing?
5. How many sides does a parallelogram have and what type of shape is it?

KEY WORDS
Make sure you understand these words before moving on!
- Scale
- Representation
- Elevation
- Planometric
- Quadrilateral
- Polygon

Isometric Projection

Isometric Projection

Isometric projection...
- can be used to produce a **3D object to scale**
- uses **30°/60° angles**.

You will need to use...
- a grid sheet to help you draw it *or*
- a 30°/60° set square.

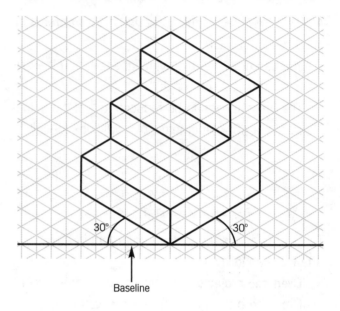

30°   30°

Baseline

Drawing Ellipses in Isometric

You can grid an ellipse shape within a square in isometric and use the red points to help plot the shape.

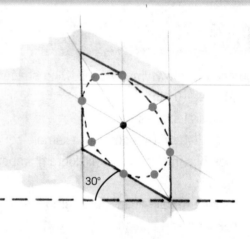

30°

Exploded Drawings

Exploded drawings are used to show how an **object fits together**.

An exploded view of an object...
- is to scale
- is accurate
- may have the **construction lines** left in to show how it has been drawn.

This type of drawing is often produced by designers and architects as it is **quicker than perspective** drawing.

An Exploded Drawing of a Pencil Sharpener

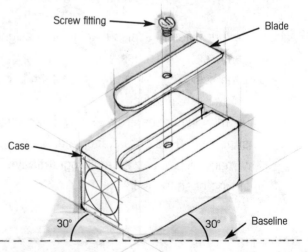

Screw fitting

Blade

Case

30°   30°   Baseline

Perspective Drawings

You can use **perspective techniques** in your design ideas and presentation. Perspective drawings use a number of points according to the view you wish to represent. They are used when showing your client how your final product will **look in reality**.

You can draw this technique on Google SketchUp, ProDesktop, 2D Design or AutoCAD® on your computer. You can produce any finish you wish and also add the direction the light is coming from.

Horizon Line and Vanishing Point

The **horizon line**…
- is also known as your **'eye line'**
- splits the sky from the ground
- has a point on it called the **vanishing point**.

All lines apart from the vertical and horizontal ones meet at the vanishing point.

One point and two point perspective has vanishing point(s) sitting on the horizon line.

There is also a three point perspective where the vanishing point is below the horizon line. This is a very complex drawing to do and one you only need to be aware of and not draw.

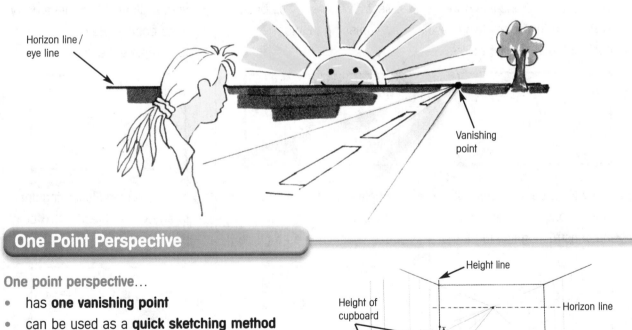

Horizon line / eye line

Vanishing point

One Point Perspective

One point perspective…
- has **one vanishing point**
- can be used as a **quick sketching method**
- is mostly used for **interiors**.

You can measure heights and depths to make your drawing look in **'proportion'**.

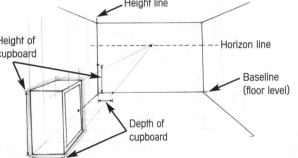

Height line

Height of cupboard

Horizon line

Baseline (floor level)

Depth of cupboard

Perspective Drawings

Two Point Perspective

Two point perspective...

- gives a **more realistic** view point than a one point perspective
- has **two vanishing points** a distance away from each other on the 'horizon line'
- can show three view points depending on where the object is in relation to the horizon line.

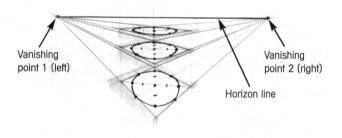

Ellipses in Two Point Perspective

Ellipses in two point perspective are plotted in a similar way to the isometric version, but the square is in perspective.

Drawing in Two Point Perspective

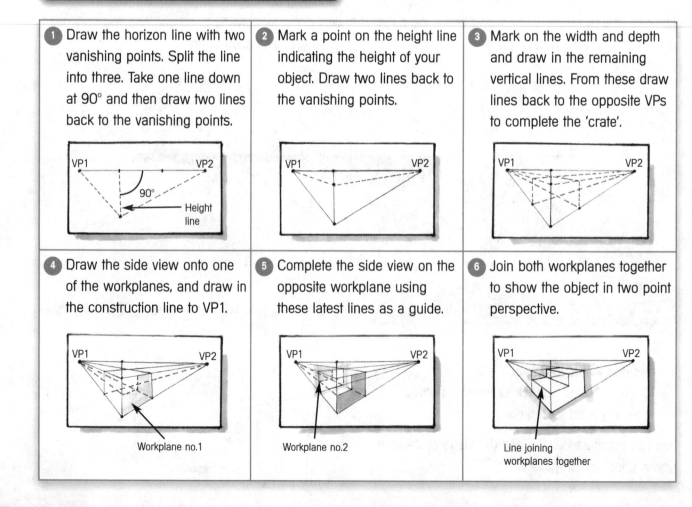

1 Draw the horizon line with two vanishing points. Split the line into three. Take one line down at 90° and then draw two lines back to the vanishing points.

2 Mark a point on the height line indicating the height of your object. Draw two lines back to the vanishing points.

3 Mark on the width and depth and draw in the remaining vertical lines. From these draw lines back to the opposite VPs to complete the 'crate'.

4 Draw the side view onto one of the workplanes, and draw in the construction line to VP1.

5 Complete the side view on the opposite workplane using these latest lines as a guide.

6 Join both workplanes together to show the object in two point perspective.

Standards in Working Drawings

Working Drawings

Designers pass detailed working drawings onto a manufacturer to make. These give the necessary **instructions for a prototype** to be built.

Each drawing has to include the following:
- accurate measurements
- assembly instructions
- specification for materials / colours and finishes.

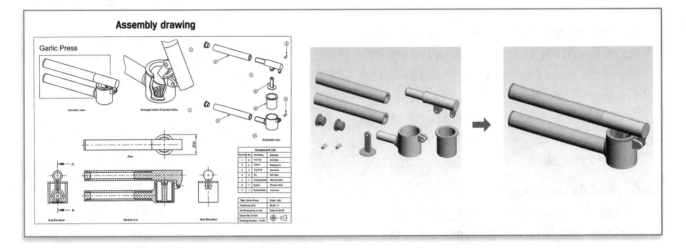

Standards for Trade

The **British Standards Institution** (**BSI**) encourages the promotion of British Standards.

It is a well-known, worldwide organisation that discusses standards in European and International committees, which are then taken on as British Standards in industry.

The following abbreviations are used:
- **BS** means the standard is a British Standard and is used mainly in the UK.
- **EN** means the standard is a European Standard and is used throughout Europe.
- **ISO** means the standard is an International Standard used throughout the world.
- **ISO 9000** has now been replaced with **ISO 9001** and relates to the quality assurance standards of a company, using set guidelines.

Quick Test

1. What is an isometric projection good for drawing?
2. What is the function of an exploded drawing?
3. What is the horizon line also known as?
4. A one point perspective gives a more realistic viewpoint than a two point perspective. True or false?
5. What does BSI stand for?

KEY WORDS

Make sure you understand these words before moving on!
- Isometric projection
- Exploded drawing
- Construction lines
- Horizon line
- Vanishing point
- Proportion
- One point perspective
- Two point perspective
- BSI

Standards in Working Drawings

Standards on Working Drawings

The **BSI** has set standards in working drawings that are recognised throughout the industry (BS 8888, 2006).

Here are some examples of basic standards for 'lines':

- **Continuous thick line** (———) – for outlines or edges (could use H or 2H for these) where only one of the faces forming an edge can be seen.
- **Continuous thin line** (———) – for projection or dimension lines (could use a 4H pencil for this).
- **Chain thin line** (-------) – for centre lines or lines of symmetry.

When using **dimensioning**…

- always use **millimetres** on your drawings
- numbers should be **written above** and in the **middle of the line**.

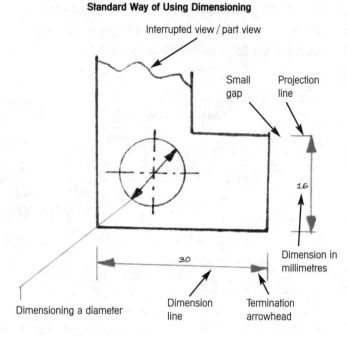

Standard Way of Using Dimensioning

Interrupted view / part view

Small gap

Projection line

16

Dimension in millimetres

30

Dimensioning a diameter

Dimension line

Termination arrowhead

Kitemark

The Kitemark is a voluntary certification scheme that is awarded by the **British Standards Institution.** The Kitemark shows that the product or service meets the relevant quality standards and has been independently tested.

The products or services are entitled to use the Kitemark with the standard number and their licence number to promote their Kitemark status.

Kitemark

™

Copyright and Patents

It's important to make sure that you have the legal rights to your product.

The **Copyright, Design and Patents Act 1988** came into force on 1 August 1989. The basic role of this Copyright Act is to restrict unauthorised copying of products and other designed items.

A company who have paid for copyright usually have the symbol, ©, next to their company name.

A **patent** protects a **new design or idea** by giving the owner the right to stop others from making, using, importing or selling the invention without their permission.

The design / idea will be registered, ®, so that you have the sole rights to use it. The word Kitemark™ and the Kitemark™ symbol are registered trademarks of BSI.

Third Angle Orthographic Projection

Third angle **orthographic projection** is the most common way of showing a working drawing. It's used to produce accurate drawings to give to a manufacturer to make.

Third angle orthographic projection shows up to four views of an object:

* **plan view**
* **front elevation**
* **two side elevations**.

The views are always set out the same way.

The third angle orthographic projection symbol is added to diagrams to help explain their layout:

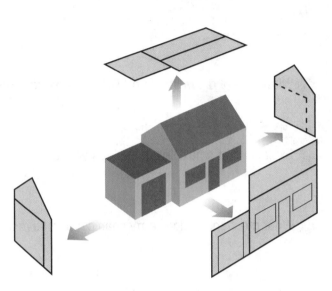

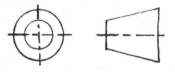

You can draw a third angle orthographic projection by hand. Remember to label the views and include all major dimensions.

Some designers still do hand drawn drawings, but **Computer Aided Design (CAD)** is more often used to produce them, so that all the information can be transferred easily to computerised machinery. You can also do your drawings using CAD.

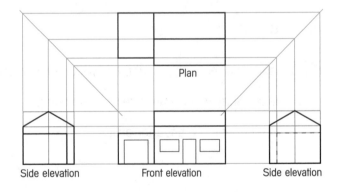

Side elevation   Front elevation   Side elevation

Quick Test

1. Where should numbers be written in relation to the dimension line?
2. Why would you patent an idea?
3. How do designers today normally produce their working drawings?
4. Name the four different views you can draw on an orthographic projection.

Practice Questions

1. What drawing tool can you use to help draw the top of a cylinder in 3D?

   ....

   ....

2. What type of drawing can a 30/60° set square help with?

   ....

3. Explain what a flexible curve helps you to do.

   ....

4. What mechanism does a mechanical pen have to propel the lead through the pen?

   ....

5. Which type of pencil is useful for drawing construction lines? Tick the correct option.

   A 2B ⬭

   B 2H ⬭

   C HB ⬭

6. Circle the correct option in the following sentence.

   Fineline / **Marker** pens are used for sketching.

7. What two pens are good for outlines?

   a) ....

   b) ....

8. What type of drawing do designers use to send to manufacturers?

   ....

9. Where is the plan view positioned on a third angle orthographic?

   ....

10 Draw lines between the boxes to match each drawing technique to the correct orientation.

Drawing Techniques   **Orientation**

Planometric	Two point
Perspective	45 / 45 degrees
Crating	No measured angle
Isometric	30 degrees

11 Give the scale ratio for a drawing, which is twice the size of the actual object.

....

12 Give three methods of enlarging images.

a) ....

b) ....

c) ....

13 How many sides does a hexagon have?

....

14 Give two benefits of drawing an exploded view in isometric.

a) ....

b) ....

15 What is the alternative name for an eye line? ....

16 What is one point perspective most commonly used for? ....

17 What is a Kitemark a symbol of?

....

18 What is the name of the organisation that issues a Kitemark?

....

....

Design and Market Influences

Influential Designs · AQA

You can gain influence in your design ideas by studying existing designers' work. You can use some of their techniques or develop their ideas to create some of your own.

Harry Beck · AQA

Harry Beck (1903–1974) was an electrical draughtsman who was aware of different colours on resistors.

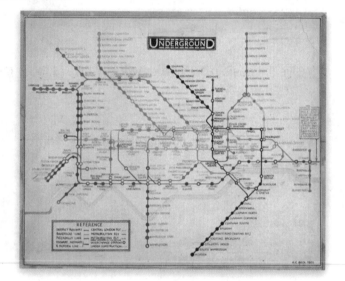

He designed a colour coded system for the **underground stations** in the 1930s. The result was a clear and comprehensible chart that would become an essential guide to London – and a template for transport maps the world over.

Beck's system is known as a **schematic map** and represents the elements of a system using **graphic symbols**. The underground map that Beck designed is for travellers to find their way from one station to another. This information is represented in a simplistic form to avoid confusion. Beck's design survives to the present day but he didn't receive official recognition for his accomplishment until the 1990s.

The Alessi Company · AQA

The **Alessi** Factory was founded in 1921 by Alberto Alessi's grandfather, and produced general **homeware items**. Alberto (born 1946) took over the company in 1970 and commissioned leading artists and architects, including Salvador Dali, Michael Graves, Aldo Rossi and Philippe Starck. Using designers from different fields in this way resulted in fresh and innovative designs, many of which are now regarded as modern classics.

Jock Kinneir and Margaret Calvert | AQA

Jock Kinneir **(1917–1974) and Margaret** Calvert **(born 1936)** designed a **signage system** of carefully coordinated lettering, colours, shapes and symbols for Britain's new motorways in the late 1950s and for all other roads in the mid 1960s. The signs were clear and functional as they could be understood quickly and accurately from a fast moving car. Their designs are a role model for modern road signage in other countries and are still in use today.

Wally Olins | AQA

Wally Olins **(born 1930)** was the co-founder of Wolff Olins until 1997. He is one of the biggest practitioners of **corporate identity** and **branding** including: BT, Prudential, Renault, Volkswagen and P&O. Olins believed that the product reflected the positive qualities of the whole company.

PRUDENTIAL

Robert Sabuda | AQA

Robert Sabuda **(born 1965)** initially worked as a package designer before illustrating his first **children's book series** of 'Bulky Board Books' in 1987. He specialises in **pop-up mechanisms** in books for which he gained recognition in 1994. Sabuda more recently produced the book *Chronicles of Narnia* by C.S. Lewis in a pop-up format.

Quick Test

1. What did Harry Beck design in the 1930s?
2. What year was the Alessi factory founded?
3. What did Kinneir and Calvert design in the 1950s?
4. What was Olins one of the biggest practitioners in?
5. What type of books is Robert Sabuda famous for?

KEY WORDS

Make sure you understand these words before moving on!

- Beck
- Schematic map
- Alessi
- Kinneir and Calvert
- Olins
- Sabuda

Design and Market Influences

Ergonomics and Anthropometrics

Ergonomics is the application of **scientific information** to the design of objects, systems and the environment, for human use. Ergonomics is an important part of research and any new product must be suited to the user, and therefore comfortable to use.

Anthropometric data is supplied by the British Standards Institution based on the **sizes of people** (more detailed data may be found in your local library). This data helps designers to design products for their target market.

For example, a designer will have used anthropometric data to decide the correct height of the chair and desk for sitting at a computer screen or the correct size and shape of the handle on a hand tool. In graphic products, you may need to consider anthropometric data relating to hand sizes, e.g. for designing packaging, greeting cards, etc. The tables give anthropometric data for the sitting position and hand sizes as shown in the illustrations. They give a range of data from the smallest to largest sizes and all measurements are in millimetres.

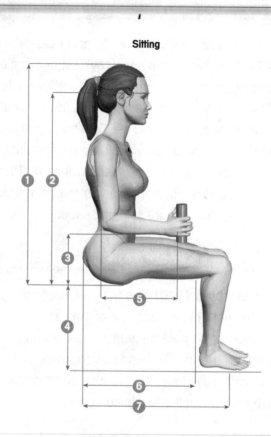

Sitting

Hand Size / Grip

Sitting	Short	Average	Tall
❶ Sitting height	795	880	965
❷ Sitting eye height	685	765	845
❸ Sitting elbow height	185	240	295
❹ Popliteal height	355	420	490
❺ Elbow-grip length	304	343	387
❻ Buttock-popliteal length	435	488	550
❼ Buttock-knee length	520	583	645

Hand size / grip	Small	Average	Large
❽ Hand length	159	182	205
❾ Palm length	89	102.5	116
❿ Thumb length	40	49	58
⓫ Index finger length	60	69.5	79
⓬ Hand breadth	69	82	95
⓭ Maximum grip diameter	43	51	59

Design and Market Influences

Design Factors

Designers consider a list of factors when designing a new product:

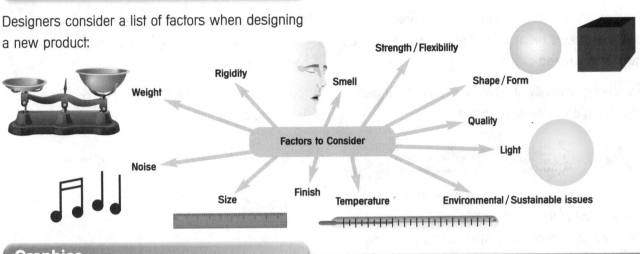

Graphics

Legibility is an important factor when designing. For example, if you look at the 'Triflora' logo, the lettering is very decorative, but difficult to read from an ergonomic point of view.

It's important that lettering is quick and **easy to read** on posters, adverts, etc. in order to sell the product.

It's also important to choose a font that has a *style* and *colour* that is easy to read – particularly for warning signs like Fire Exits.

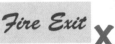

Contrast means that **one colour can stand out from another** and is an important ergonomic factor. If the contrast is wrong, writing can be hard to read.

A significant minority of the population are red / green *colour blind*, so this should also be taken into account when designing a product.

EASY TO READ ✓

✗

Quick Test

1. List three factors to consider when designing a new product.
2. What is colour contrast?
3. What is anthropometric data?
4. Where is a good place to find anthropometric data?
5. What units of measurement should always be used in anthropometric data?

KEY WORDS
Make sure you understand these words before moving on!
- Ergonomics
- Anthropometric data
- Style
- Colour
- Contrast
- Colour blind

Product Analysis

Product Analysis

Product analysis is about **looking at a product, disassembling it** (even taking it apart) and working out **how it was made**.

By looking carefully at a product you are not only evaluating it but learning from it.

It also helps to establish if there's a 'gap in the market', so you can design something to suit a particular problem.

You need to consider a list of categories when analysing a product.

1. Function

When thinking about a product's function think about '**what is the need for this product?**' You can use diagrams to demonstrate how it's used and to explain its purpose.

For example, when evaluating milk, its functions could be...
- for eating with breakfast cereal, or as a drink
- for providing calcium to strengthen bones.

2. Cost

When analysing a product, you need to look at its cost and **compare prices**. For example, how much does the product cost individually or in bulk?

Built-in obsolescence is the process of a product becoming **obsolete** or breaking down after a period

of use. This is of benefit to the manufacturer, as it guarantees that people will want to buy the product again.

You also need to be aware of the **social costs** involved in packaging, i.e. costs that affect the community, such as waste disposal.

3. Target Market

You need to ask various questions when finding out who the target market is for a particular product:
- **Who uses this product** and how do you know? (A questionnaire is a good idea.)
- Are different styles used for different **age groups**, **cultures** and **religions**?
- Use **line graphs**, **bar charts**, **pie charts** and **pictographs** to record results and analyse them.

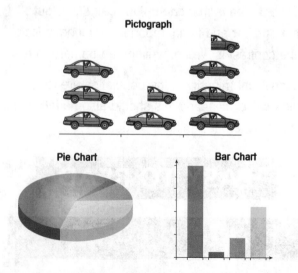

4. Moral and Cultural Issues

It's important that you consider the views of different cultures when designing a product. Some colours or principles can offend religious or cultural groups of people.

Materials and components for a product should be sourced (as much as possible) from both **ethical** and **recyclable** sources. The manufacture of the products should be made in good working conditions. Disabilities sometimes need to be considered too.

There is an increased importance for international trade (**globalisation of products**), which means that different cultures and their environments need to be considered.

A trade body such as the ETI (**Ethical Trading Initiative**) is formed from all types of businesses that promote social and environmental fair trade.

5. Product History

When analysing a product, you also need to consider where the product originates from. Use diagrams (using dates / events where possible) to explain the evolution of the product.

First milk bottles – 1880s   **First paper milk cartons – Early 1900s**   **First plastic milk containers – 1960s**

6. Alternative Products

You need to evaluate your product against either a similar or a competitive product. How do they compare on price, shape, form, use, etc.?

The table shows a comparison of a cardboard carton against a plastic container.

Carton		Container	
• Packaging is difficult to open • Difficult to reseal • Can be easily thrown away with household rubbish		• Easy to open and reseal • Bulky in transportation • Can be reused for other purposes (not food products) and recycled	

7. Hygiene

It's important to consider hygiene when analysing a product. For example, will it be easy for the end user to clean? It's helpful to compare your product with other similar products.

Harmful bacteria are the most common cause of illness from raw meat, fruit and vegetables if they are not stored or washed sufficiently. Food poisoning can result from inappropriate storage or cleanliness of a kitchen.

Product Analysis

8. Ergonomics

When analysing a product you need to think about **ergonomics**, i.e. how the product suits the user.

For example, when designing a milk carton the stages of pouring milk from the carton should be discussed:

- Look at how the hand grips the handle on the bottle.
- Describe how the bottle top is taken off.
- When pouring, how heavy is it to lift and which parts of the body enable this function to happen?

9. The Manufacturing Process

You need to explain what method of production is used to make your product and why (using diagrams).

You also need to say whether it is mass / batch or a one-off production, as this has an effect on the costings.

Mass / batch production is **large scale** manufacturing of a product. For example, a milk container is a continuous mass produced product.

One-off production is where **one product** is produced at any one time, often to test as a prototype, before deciding the type of manufacture it will be.

10. Materials

When analysing a product you also need to investigate what material(s) your product is made from:

- What are the origins and properties of each material?
- Why is that material used?
- It should also be compared against another similar product.

HDPE

Glass

Aluminium

The 6 'R's in Recycling

Sustainability is about redesigning the ways that we meet the needs and wants of society, without depleting resources or harming natural cycles for future generations. These need to be maintained to preserve the **environment**.

There are six points you need to consider from a sustainability point of view when designing a product:

R	Description
Reduce	• Reduce waste – use less material to produce a product. • Prevent waste – use processes that create less waste. • Consider Life Cycle Analysis, i.e. the length of time a product is used without fault and the effect this has on the environment.
Reuse	• Reuse bags, containers, paper, boxes and other items, and avoid single-use items. • Donate or re-sell items to charity shops or organisations in need.
Recycle	• Keep raw materials in the system, try to be less dependent on natural resources. • Keep recycling products – it reduces the amount of material going into landfill, and reduces the necessity for mining and chopping down trees. • Buy recycled products and help create a larger demand for them – more demand means more manufacturers selling more recycled products.
Refuse	• Refuse to buy goods that cannot easily be recycled.
Repair	• Repair items rather than buying a new one – it often costs less too! • Repair items and save on the manufacturing costs of a brand new product.
Rethink	• Think how you could approach your design problems differently, considering the other 5 'R's.

Quick Test

1. What part of the body do you need measurements for when looking at the handles on a milk carton?
2. What is the term for the group of people who will buy or use an end product?
3. Other than plastic, name two materials that you can take to a recycling bank.
4. What does the term 'sustainability' mean?

KEY WORDS

Make sure you understand these words before moving on!

- Function
- Cost
- Built-in obsolescence
- Target market
- Originate
- Mass/batch production
- One-off production
- Sustainability
- Environment

The Environment

Product Design and the Environment

Eco-design is the consideration of **environmental issues** in the design and development of products or services. New designs are created to produce less waste and damage to the environment.

All stages of a product's life cycle are considered, for example...

- during its production / manufacture
- during its use
- after its use / disposal.

Materials and the Environment

Biodegradable materials are organic substances which are **broken down naturally** and absorbed into the environment over a period of time, e.g. a banana skin.

Non-biodegradable products, which are often synthetic, can't be broken down naturally. They are usually taken to **landfill sites** to be disposed of.

Landfill sites are where local authorities and industry take waste to be buried and compacted with other wastes under the ground. **The Environment Agency** licenses and regulates landfill sites to ensure that their impact on the environment is minimised.

The Ecological Footprint

The **ecological footprint** is a measure of human demand on the Earth's natural resources. It represents the total area of the planet's surface that would be needed to replace the resources consumed by an individual and absorb the waste they produce.

The footprint is broken down to show the contributing factors to help identify which activities have the greatest impact. It is then used to estimate how many planet Earths would be needed to support the entire human population if everybody shared such a lifestyle.

A **carbon footprint** is a similar measurement. It assesses the impact that human activities have on the environment in terms of the amount of **carbon dioxide** produced.

An Example Ecological Footprint

Personal Care · Food · Travel and Transport · Other · Home

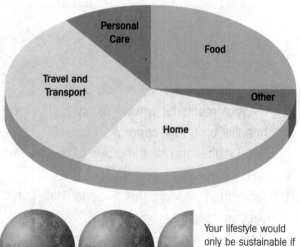

Your lifestyle would only be sustainable if there were 2.46 planets to support us.

Energy Sources Edexcel

Most of the energy traditionally used in industry comes from fossil fuels, e.g. coal, oil and gas. These are **non-renewable** energy sources, because they can't be replaced in a lifetime and **will eventually run out.**

Renewable energy sources are those that will not run out, i.e. they are **continually available**.

The **Kyoto Protocol** has set up legally binding commitments **to reduce the level of greenhouse gas emissions** in the atmosphere and encourage the use of renewable energy sources.

Renewable Energy Sources Edexcel

Source	How it Works	
Wind turbines	The kinetic energy in wind can be used to produce 'clean' electricity using wind turbines. The wind turns the blades on the turbine, which drives a generator to produce electricity.	
Solar cells and panels	Solar **cells** and **panels** are made of a **silicon material** that captures heat energy. This is then converted into electrical energy. The three categories of silicon cells are monocrystalline, polycrystalline and amorphous silicon.	
Biomass / Biofuels	**Biomass** is most often referred to as **organic matter**, like timber and crops, which are specifically grown to create power and heat. **Biofuels** are the **fuels** that are produced from biomass.	

Quick Test

1. A biodegradable product can't be broken down naturally. True or false?
2. What is a non-biodegradable product?
3. Where are non-biodegradable products usually disposed of?
4. What is kinetic energy?

KEY WORDS
Make sure you understand these words before moving on!
- Biodegradable
- Non-biodegradable
- Ecological footprint
- Kinetic energy
- Solar
- Biofuel

Practice Questions

1. What two things could you do to reuse products?

   a) .... b) ....

2. List the six 'R's.

   a) .... b) ....

   c) .... d) ....

   e) .... f) ....

3. Explain what a landfill site is.

   ....

   ....

4. a) What does biodegradable mean?

   ....

   ....

   b) Name one biodegradable graphic product.

   ....

5. What do solar cells capture?

   ....

6. Name three renewable energy sources.

   a) ....

   b) ....

   c) ....

7. Explain what an ecological footprint is.

   ....

   ....

8. What is the name of the organisation that licences and regulates landfill sites?

   ....

9 Explain what a carbon footprint is.

10 What did Harry Beck develop that is still used today in London?

11 a) What did Alberto Alessi introduce in his company from the 1970s?

b) Name two of these from your answer to part a).

i) _____ ii) _____

12 Who designed a signage system for Britain's new motorways in the 1950s? Tick the two correct options.

A Robert Sabuda ◯ **B** Margaret Calvert ◯

C Jock Kinneir ◯ **D** Wally Olins ◯

13 What is a schematic map?

14 Is the following statement **true** or **false**?

Anthropometric data is the study of the human brain.

15 Explain what a target market is.

16 What is built-in obsolescence?

17 Explain what product analysis is.

Modelling

The following materials are used for building a **prototype** of a design. Each material has different functions and properties. These materials can help to create shapes or forms to represent what the product could look like.

Material	Functions and Properties
Corrugated plastic sheet	• Layered plastic with two thin sheets on the outer skin and a fluted centre • Used in high quality packaging • Not suitable for moulding, e.g. vacuum forming
Blockfoam / Styrofoam™	• A dense version of polystyrene • Can be cut and moulded easily • Glued together using PVA • Can be paint finished with emulsion or poster paint • Can be used as plaster-based fillers (for filling gaps) which is sanded down on the surface to whatever shape you require on your model
Foam board	• A laminate of thin foam sandwiched between thin board • Available in different thicknesses • Expensive • Often used for architectural modelling
Hard wax	• Wax that is melted down and reformed into a mould • Difficult to mould dry as it has a crumbly texture
Plaster bandage	• Used wet onto a wire mesh or other surface • Creates sculptural shapes in layers • Hardens when dry, allowing it to be sanded smooth
Acrylic	• Used for modelling, but difficult to cut, form and join together • A very brittle thermoplastic material • Available in a range of different thicknesses and colours
Medium density fibre board (MDF)	• A manufactured fibreboard with no grain • Uniform, consistent quality and readily available • Glued together when necessary using PVA glue • A very absorbent material that needs to be sealed first • Most useful at thicknesses 3, 6 and 9mm
Jelutong and Balsa	• Hardwoods that are used for modelling • Jelutong is low density, has a straight grain and a fine texture. • Balsa is a soft hardwood that is easy to shape and mould.
Board	• Comes in a variety of thicknesses, sizes and colours • Most commonly used as a material for modelling

Adhesives for Model Making

Rubber-based cement...

- is a rubber-based adhesive
- should be applied to each surface for 10 minutes before bringing the surfaces together
- is good for mounting photographs and allows time for repositioning
- has a strong smell
- is safe to use but you need to be in a well-ventilated room.

Glue stick...

- is a glue which bonds paper to paper
- creates a weak bond, but is commonly used as it's cheap
- is safe to use and environmentally-friendly.

Aerosol adhesive (also known as spray mount) is...
- useful for sticking pieces of paper together
- also used as a 'photo mount', designed to stick photos onto your work
- quite toxic so you need to wear a mask when spraying and make sure the room is well-ventilated.

Polyvinyl acetate (PVA) is...
- known as either Resin W™ or Unibond™ which bonds wood or card
- a white adhesive but dries colourless and sets in three hours and hardens in 24 hours
- safe to use, but avoid contact with your eyes.

Balsa cement is...
- an ideal glue to use on balsa wood
- quick-setting
- safe to use but you need to be in a well-ventilated room and use eye protection.

Epoxy resin...
- is known as Araldite®, which is a two part adhesive
- creates a strong bond within 4–5 minutes and hardening takes place over 2–3 hours
- is safe to use but you must wear a safety mask and work in a well-ventilated room
- should not come in prolonged contact with the skin.

Acrylic cement...
- is known as Tensol no. 12® and welds acrylic together
- should be used in a well-ventilated room and eye protection worn.

Glue guns...
- are heated up electronically – this softens the glue through the nozzle, which then cools quickly and sets
- are useful in model making
- should be used carefully as the hot glue can burn if it comes into contact with your skin.

Quick Test

1. What is the centre of corrugated plastic called?
2. What are the alternative names for PVA glue?
3. Name one disadvantage of acrylic.
4. Name one disadvantage of foam board.
5. Name two functions of an aerosol adhesive.
6. Fill in the missing words:
   Aerosol adhesive is also known as

   _____

KEY WORDS
Make sure you understand these words before moving on!
- Corrugated plastic sheet
- Hard wax
- Balsa
- MDF
- Adhesive
- PVA
- Epoxy resin

Modelling

A **fixative** is a spray which **prevents loose particles** and smudging of your drawing as the spray seals the particles. A fixative…

- is used to fix soft pencils or pastels to card or paper
- comes in an aerosol can (a cheap alternative is hairspray)
- should be used in a well-ventilated room with a mask.

Other fixings include **double-sided** and **single-sided tape**, **velcro**®, double-sided sticky **pads** and **staples**.

Masking comes in three forms and is used in airbrushing and pastel techniques:

- **Sheet** masking is self-adhesive. You use a scalpel to cut out shapes and stick onto paper.
- **Tape** masking is used to mask off small areas.
- **Fluid** masking is applied with a brush to very intricate areas, allowed to dry, then peeled off.

You must be careful when using a knife and where possible use a **safety ruler**.

Tools

Die cutters are made of metal and are used to punch holes into cardboard or paper (they are like pastry cutters). You can buy die cutters in different shapes. Cardboard packaging is cut from big industrial die cutters.

A **scalpel** / **craft knife** is a sharp knife used for cutting card. It's used with a **safety ruler**.

Compass cutters and **circle cutters** can be used to cut circles in paper or thin card. **Rotary cutters** can be used to cut straight lines. A **perforation cutter** can be used to create a perforated edge.

A **guillotine** is used to cut paper or card in paper / packaging industries. In school, you would use a paper trimmer or rotary trimmer.

A **scroll saw** (fret saw) is good at cutting wood and plastics into intricate shapes. It's similar to a coping saw, which is a hand held tool that cuts wood at different angles.

A **creasing bar** is a machine that creates creases in cardboard to give an accurate fold. Creasing retains the strength of a material whereas scoring seriously weakens it.

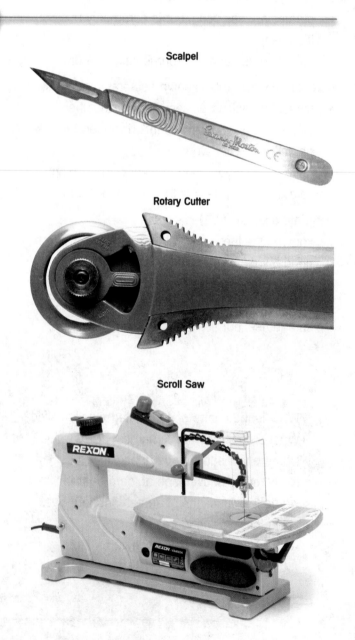

Scalpel

Rotary Cutter

Scroll Saw

Finishes
Edexcel • AQA

Encapsulation is when paper is **sealed by heat** in a pocket or pouch.

Lamination is a **layered composite** of several materials, e.g. Tetra Pak™ liquid containers are made of varnish, paper and aluminium foil.

Mounting / picture framing:

- The cardboard used to mount or frame pictures is often known as '**mounting board**'.
- The sheets are measured by thickness in microns and are usually from 100–1500 microns thick.
- The picture is attached from behind the window of the card using masking tape.

Fillers:

- Plaster or body fillers can be used to fill gaps in your model.
- These can be sanded down to achieve a smooth finish after the plaster is dry.

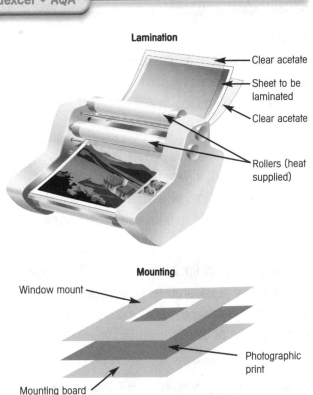

Lamination
- Clear acetate
- Sheet to be laminated
- Clear acetate
- Rollers (heat supplied)

Mounting
- Window mount
- Photographic print
- Mounting board

Paints and Inks
Edexcel • AQA

Lacquers / varnishes:

- Consist of a **synthetic resin** (acrylic and cellulose), dissolved in an organic solvent.
- Evaporate to give a quick drying paint.
- Come in different finishes, e.g. gloss, matt, satin, coloured and clear.

Oil-based gloss:

- Used to create a shiny finish.
- Uses a medium of natural drying oil called linseed.
- Durable and waterproof.

Quick Test

1. What do die cutters resemble?
2. What shape does a compass cutter cut?
3. The alternative method of folding card, instead of using a creasing bar, is what?
4. When a picture is heat sealed in a pocket or pouch, what is the process known as?
5. What type of finish does an oil-based gloss have?

KEY WORDS

Make sure you understand these words before moving on!

- Fixative
- Die cutter
- Rotary cutter
- Creasing bar
- Encapsulation
- Lamination
- Mounting board

Modelling

Paints and Inks (cont.) Edexcel • AQA

Emulsions…
- contain vinyl or acrylic resin
- are water based
- are not waterproof.

Inks…
- come in three types – water soluble, water resistant and solvent based
- are most commonly used as water soluble inks
- are mostly used in printing, not necessarily model making.

Health and safety tip: Always protect your lungs with a safety mask and clean brushes and rags after use or dispose of them. You should wear a barrier cream or gloves to protect your skin.

Pre-manufactured Components AQA • OCR

Click fasteners / clic rivets…
- comprise two-part plastic rivets
- **bind** two sheets of materials together, e.g. styrene or coroflute
- are available in different lengths for various sheet thicknesses
- fix together with a 'clic' sound
- are very difficult to take apart once pushed together.

Eyelets…
- fasten onto sheet material to reinforce a hole
- are sometimes referred to as **grommets**
- often come in brass and are in two parts which can be hand pressed together using 'die cutters'.

Paper fasteners…
- are used to attach two pieces of paper or cardboard through a hole made by a hole punch
- can be used to simulate mechanical movement of two parts.

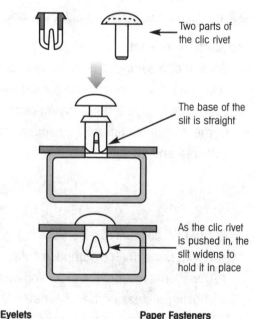

How a Plastic Rivet Works

Two parts of the clic rivet

The base of the slit is straight

As the clic rivet is pushed in, the slit widens to hold it in place

Eyelets   Paper Fasteners

Pre-manufactured Components (cont.)   AQA • OCR

Velcro®...

* is a brand name for **hook and loop fasteners**
* has looped material on one side and a series of hooks on the other which attach together when the surfaces touch.

Pressfit...

* relies on the tensile and compression strengths of the materials to 'fit' together
* works by **friction** resulting in the parts staying together, e.g. metal bearings and water tight connectors.

Double-sided sticky pads...

* are made of **foam** which has a **self-adhesive** surface on both sides
* are useful for sticking cardboard together, especially in modelling.

Double-sided tape...

* is transparent tape that has **self-adhesive** surfaces on both sides
* is useful for sticking cardboard together, especially in modelling.

Hook and Loop Fastening

Pressfit Connectors

Double-sided Tape

Quick Test

1. What are the three types of inks called?
2. What two forces does pressfit use to fit materials together?
3. What are eyelets used for?
4. What kind of movement is simulated by fixing a paper fastener onto cardboard?

KEY WORDS

Make sure you understand these words before moving on!

* Clic rivets
* Bind
* Eyelets
* Velcro®
* Pressfit

Smart and Modern Materials

Smart and Modern Materials

Smart materials respond to **changes in their environment**, e.g. temperature and light. Some smart materials also have a 'memory', i.e. they can return to their original state. **Modern materials** are developed through the invention of **new or improved processes**.

Smart / Modern Material	Properties and Uses
Thermochromic materials	• Respond to changes in **temperature** by changing colour • Made of liquid crystals or metal compounds • Used for t-shirts, temptoos (temporary tattoos), mugs and temperature strips
Photochromic materials	• Change colour in response to changes in **light intensity** • Used for spectacle lenses and 'smart' windows for cars and coaches
Liquid Crystal Displays (LCD)	• Display that consists of two transparent panels and a liquid crystal surface in between. Voltage is applied to certain areas, causing the crystal to turn black. • Light source behind the panels transmits through transparent crystals, but mostly blocked by dark crystals • Used for TV screens
Phosphorescent materials	• Also known as **'afterglow'** or **'glow in the dark'** materials • Produce visible or invisible light • Function by absorbing light when exposed to a light source • Can be applied to materials as a paint or spray form • Available in both water-based and solvent-based mediums
Precious metal clays	• A clay with a metal content. When it dries, it needs to be heated to set • Used to make beads for jewellery and for small sculptures
Paper foam / Potatopak	• Biodegradable, disposable trays, plates, bowls, cups and containers that are made from potato starch • Guaranteed not to last − after use they can be composted or used for pig food or in a worm farm
Polymorph	• A thermoplastic material that can be shaped and reshaped • Supplied as granules and can be used in the classroom. Shaped by hand or pressed into shape using a mould • Expensive, but suitable for 3D modelling
Electronic paper displays (EPDs)	• Used for displaying digital versions of books and e-paper magazines, bus time tables and electronic billboards
Transdermal prescription drug patches	• External patches, which stick to the skin to infuse drugs into the body

New Materials

Nanotechnology

Nanotechnology deals with materials at an **atomic** or **molecular** scale and is being used to create products that are lighter, stronger, cleaner, less expensive and more precise. It can be used for the following:

- Food packaging with added anti-microbial agents.
- Increasing the strength of polymers to replicate properties of metals and making surfaces harder wearing.
- Clothing that repels dirt, stains and body odours and can 'self-clean' with a cup of water.
- Garments that can sense, react and absorb an impact or collision and so protect your body. These can be used in extreme sports or military applications.
- Sports clothing that can measure your fitness levels and create individual training programmes based on your body's feedback.

Carbon Fibres

Carbon fibres can be woven into a fabric sheet and then impregnated with an epoxy or phenolic resin and forced into a mould. The material is then cured (or set) with heated steam to create a very **strong lightweight material**, used for example in Formula One racing cars, aircraft and bicycles.

Quick Test

1. What material is often used to make beads for jewellery?
2. Thermochromic materials change colour by a change in what?
3. Photochromic materials change colour by a change in what?
4. Give one use of carbon fibres.
5. Name the material that is also known as 'afterglow'.

KEY WORDS

Make sure you understand these words before moving on!
- Smart materials
- Thermochromic
- Photochromic
- Phosphorescent
- Nanotechnology
- Carbon fibres

Types of Plastics

Plastics

Plastics can be used for a wide variety of products and are manufactured using a process known as **polymerisation**. Polymerisation occurs when **monomers** join together to form long chains of molecules called **polymers**.

There are two different types of plastic:
- **Thermosetting plastics**
- **Thermoplastics**.

Additives can be added to both thermoplastics and thermosetting plastics to make the quality of the material different:
- **Stabilisers** prevent moisture or UV light affecting the surface.
- **Lubricants** – sulphides and waxes make the polymer easier to form and self-lubricating in use.
- **Pigments** add colour to the plastic.
- **Plasticisers** make the plastic less brittle.
- **Anti-static agents** prevent the build up of electrical charges.

Thermosetting Plastics

Thermosetting plastics…
- are **heated** and moulded into shape
- **will not soften if re-heated** as the monomers are interlinked
- have individual monomers joined together to form a **massive polymer**.

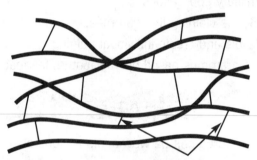

Strong links between chains stops movement between them

Types of Thermosetting Plastics

Melamine Formaldehyde, MF (Melamine Methanal) is a thermosetting plastic and heat resistant polymer. It's used for tableware, electrical installations, synthetic resin paints, decorative laminates and worktops.

Epoxy Resin, ER (Epoxide) is a resin and a hardener mixed to produce a cast for castings, printed circuit boards (PCBs) and surface coating.

Polyester Resin (PR) polymerises at room temperature and is a resin and hardener mixed together. It's often reinforced with glass fibre. It's laminated and used to form glass reinforced plastic (GRP) castings, encapsulations, car bodies and boats.

Phenol formaldehyde (Phenol methanal or bakelite) is a hard, brittle plastic, which has a dark colour, a gloss finish and is resistant to heat. It's used for dark-coloured electrical fittings and parts for domestic appliances, bottle tops and kettle / iron / saucepan handles.

Urea formaldehyde is a colourless polymer, which is coloured with artificial pigments to produce a wide range of different colours. It's used for door handles, cupboard handles, bottle tops, electrical switches and electrical fittings.

Thermoplastics

Thermoplastics…
- will soften when they're heated and can be shaped when hot
- will harden when cooled but **will soften if heated up again** and can be reshaped
- are recyclable.

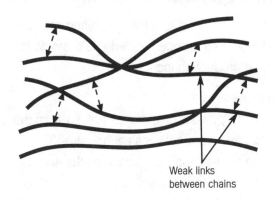

Weak links between chains

Types of Thermoplastics

HDPE Polyethylene (High Density) is a stiff, strong plastic that softens at between 120°C and 130°C. It's used for pipes, bowls, milk crates and buckets. It's also known by its trade name, polythene.

LDPE Polyethylene (Low Density) is weaker, softer and more flexible than HDPE. It's used for packaging, film, carrier bags, toys and 'squeezy' detergent bottles.

Polypropylene (PP) is a high impact strength plastic which softens at 150°C and can be flexed many times without breaking. It's used for bottle crates, medical equipment, syringes, food containers, boxes, nets and storage.

Acrylic (Polymethyl-Methacrylate) has the trade name of Perspex®. It has a glass-like transparency or opaqueness and can't be coloured with pigments. It's hard-wearing and will not shatter. It's used for display signs, baths, roof lights and machine guards.

Nylon is a hard material that has a good resistance to wear and tear. Solid nylon has low friction qualities and a high melting point. It's used for curtain rail fittings, combs, hinges, bearings, clothes and gear wheels.

PVC rigid (Polyvinyl chloride) is stiff and hard-wearing. A plasticiser can be added to create a softer more rubbery material. It's used for air and water pipes, chemical tanks, shoe soles, shrink and blister packaging, and floor and wall coverings.

Acetate film is used for packaging, printing and overlays. Film is available in finishes including clear, matt and prepared (gel coated).

Polystyrene (PS) ranges from low to high density according to its function. A low density plastic is good at absorbing shock and higher density polystyrenes are good for insulation. It can be soft and spongy and it can also be hard and brittle, depending on its density and use.

Polystyrene

Industrial Processes

Injection Moulding

Injection moulding is a manufacturing process where plastics can be injected into a mould to make a product shape.

The process is as follows:

1. Plastic powder or granules are fed from the **hopper** into a hollow steel barrel.

2. The heaters melt the plastic as the screw moves it along towards the mould.

3. Once sufficient melted plastic has accumulated, the hydraulic system forces the plastic into the mould.

4. Pressure is maintained on the mould, until it has cooled enough to be opened.

Typical materials used in injection moulding are...

- polystyrene
- polyethylene
- polypropylene
- nylon.

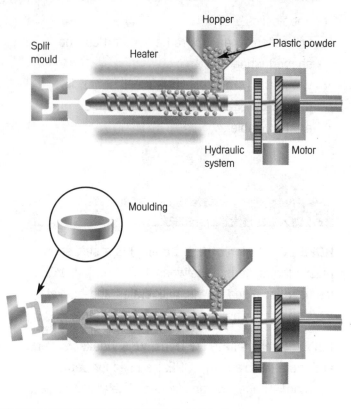

Extrusion

Extrusion is a process similar to injection moulding, but where the plastic is pushed through a mould to create 'rod-like' continuous shapes.

Typical materials used in this process are...

- polyethylene
- polyvinyl chloride
- nylon.

The process is as follows:

1. Plastic granules are fed into the hopper by the rotating screw.

2. The plastic granules are heated as they are fed through. The difference between the injection moulding process and the extrusion process is that the softened plastic is forced through a die in a continuous stream, to create long tube or sectional extrusions.

3. The extrusions are then passed through a cooling chamber.

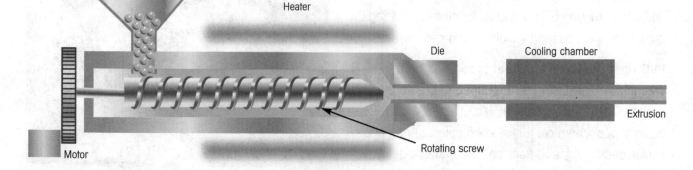

FREE

Controlled Assessment Guide

ESSENTIALS

GCSE Design & Technology
Graphic Products
Controlled Assessment Guide

About this Guide

The new GCSE Design & Technology courses are assessed through…
*   written exam papers
*   controlled assessment.

This guide provides…
*   an overview of how your course is assessed
*   an explanation of controlled assessment
*   advice on how best to demonstrate your knowledge and skills in the controlled assessment.

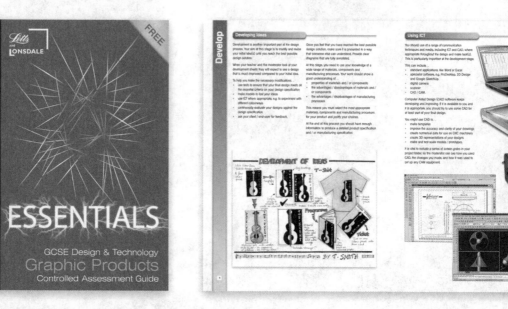

What is Controlled Assessment?

Controlled assessment has replaced coursework. It involves completing a 'design and make' task (two tasks for OCR) within a set number of hours.

Your exam board will provide you with a range of tasks to choose from. The purpose of the task(s) is to see how well you can bring all your skills and knowledge together to design and make an original product.

You must produce individual work under controlled conditions, i.e. under the supervision of a teacher.

Your teacher can review your work and give you general feedback. However, all the work must be your own.

How is Controlled Assessment Marked?

Your teacher will mark your work using guidelines from the exam board. A moderator at the exam board will review these marks to ensure that they are fair.

You will not just be marked on the quality of your end product – the other stages of design and development are just as important, if not more so!

This means it is essential to clearly communicate what you did, how you did it, and why you did it, at each stage of the task(s). You will be marked on the clarity of your communication too.

Contents

This guide looks at the main stages you will need to go through in your controlled assessment task(s), providing helpful advice and tips along the way:

Exam Board	Course	Written Paper	Controlled Assessment
AQA	Full Course	• 2 hours • 120 marks • 40% of total marks Section A (30 marks) – A design question based on a context which you will be notified of before the exam Section B (90 marks) – Covers all the content on the specification, i.e. all the material covered in your Essentials Revision Guide. *N.B. One of the questions on the written paper will carry Quality of Written Communication (QWC) marks.*	• Approx. 45 hours • 90 marks • 60% of total marks
Edexcel	Full Course	• 1 hour 30 minutes • 80 marks • 40% of total marks	• Approx. 40 hours • 100 marks • 60% of total marks The 'design and make' activities can be linked (combined design and make) or separate (design one product, make another).
OCR	Short Course and Full Course (Year 1)	**Unit A532 Sustainable Design:** • 1 hour • 60 marks • 20% of total marks (40% of short course) Section A: 15 short-answer questions. Section B: 3 questions requiring answers that may involve sketching, annotation, short sentences or more extended writing.	**Unit A531 Introduction to Design and Making:** • 20 hours • 60 marks • 30% of total marks (60% of short course)
	Full Course (Year 2)	**Unit A534 Technical Aspects of Designing and Making:** • 1 hour 15 minutes • 60 marks • 20% of total marks Section A – 3 questions based on the technical aspects of working with materials, tools and equipment. Section B – 2 questions on the design of products reflecting the wider issues of sustainability and human use. One of these questions will require a design response.	**Unit A533 Making Quality Products:** • 20 hours • 60 marks • 30% of total marks

How Your Course is Assessed

Important Considerations

Unlike your teacher, the moderator will not have the opportunity to see how you progress with the task. They will not be able to talk to you or ask questions – they must make their assessment based only on the evidence you provide. This means that it is essential to communicate your thoughts, ideas and decisions clearly at each stage of the process:

- Organise your folder so the work is in a logical order.
- Ensure that text is legible and that spelling, punctuation and grammar are accurate.
- Use an appropriate form and style of writing.
- Make sure you use technical terms correctly.

Because you only have a limited amount of time, it is essential to plan ahead. The table below gives suggested times for each of the stages.

Remember, these stages are all part of a continuous process, so these times are guidelines only based on the mark allocation and you should produce your own more detailed time plan. You need to divide the total time for each stage between the individual tasks to ensure that you spend the majority of your time working on the areas that are worth the most marks.

At the end of the controlled assessment you will need to submit the final product (or a photograph of it) along with a concise design folder. You should aim to produce about 20 x A3 sheets for your folder (10 for a short course or for separate design and make tasks). An equivalent amount of A4 sheets or electronic files may be acceptable – check with your teacher.

AQA award up to 6 marks for clarity of presentation throughout your folder. Whilst these marks are important, 84 of the total 90 marks are for the content, so make good use of your time – don't waste time creating elaborate borders and titles!

Stage	Tasks	AQA Marks	AQA Guideline Time (Hr)	OCR Unit A531 Marks	OCR Unit A531 Guideline Time (Hr)	OCR Unit A533 Marks	OCR Unit A533 Guideline Time (Hr)	Edexcel Marks	Edexcel Guideline Time (Hr)
Investigate	Analysing the brief	8	4					15	5
	Research								
	Design specification								
Design	Initial ideas	32	16	24	8	16	5	20	7
	Reviewing ideas								
Develop	Developing ideas							15	8
Plan	Product specification							6	2
	Production plan								
Make	Making product	32	16	28	9	36	12	38	16
Test and evaluate	Testing and evaluation	12	6	8	3	8	3	6	2
Communicate*	Clarity of communication	6	3	0	0	0	0	0	0
Total		90	45	60	20	60	20	100	40

Analysing the Task

To get the maximum marks, you need to…
*   analyse the task / brief in detail
*   clearly identify all the design needs.

It is a good idea to start by writing out the task / brief…
*   as it is written by the exam board
*   in your own words (to make sure you understand what you're being asked to do).

Highlight the key words and phrases and make sure you understand them.

At this stage, it is a good idea to…
*   eliminate any information that isn't important
*   identify any specific issues that need to be investigated further before you can start designing the product
*   make a list of all the questions that you need to answer before you can begin designing
*   decide what method of research is needed to answer each question.

Ask yourself the following questions:
*   Who will use the end product?
*   What will it be used for?
*   Where will it be used?
*   What sort of shop / retail outlet will it be sold through?
*   Are there any cost restrictions that will influence my design?
*   How many products would be made if it went into commercial production?

You do not need to write an essay. You could use…
*   an attribute analysis table
*   a mind map
*   a spider diagram
*   a list of bullet points.

Research

Because you don't have very long to conduct your research, you need to make sure it is all relevant.

It should help you to answer all the questions that you identified in your task analysis, so these are the areas to focus on.

Make sure you keep accurate records. You will need to refer back to the information throughout the task.

You should know about the different research methods used in commercial design, but be aware that they may not be appropriate to your design task because of the limited time available to you.

Possibly the most useful types of research that you can carry out in the limited time available to you is…
- a client / end-user interview
- product analysis.

Interviews, Questionnaires and Surveys

Interviews, questionnaires and surveys normally rely on a large sample group to produce reliable data.

You will need to adapt these methods for your design task, e.g. a single client interview or a simple questionnaire at the end of the task to evaluate your outcome.

This is fine, as long as you show that you understand the pros and cons of doing this in your evaluation.

Questions for client / end-user:
- What product do you want?
- What do you want the product to do?
- How and where will you use it?
- What size do you want?
- What style do you want?
- What do you like and dislike about existing products?

Product Analysis

The purpose of product analysis is to help you produce a product that is better than those already available. It should help you to identify…

- desirable / successful features (features you could incorporate into your design)
- undesirable / unsuccessful features (features to avoid in your design)
- areas for improvement (areas that you should try to improve upon in your design, e.g. reducing cost, making the product sustainable).

When analysing existing products, you need to identify…

- the end-user of the product
- where the product is used
- where the product is sold
- how the product works and fits together
- the possible manufacturing systems and processes used to produce it
- the materials used

- the cost
- the way graphics are used to promote the product
- what information is given on the packaging
- why a particular type of packaging has been used.

It is a good idea to show your client / end-user(s) the products too. Find out…

- what they like about them
- what they don't like about them
- whether they are good value for money
- what improvements they would like to see.

You should also consider…

- the life cycle of the product
- whether the product can be recycled
- the effect of the product on our lifestyle
- whether the product is inclusive (or whether some groups of people won't be able to use it).

Research Summary

It is essential to summarise your conclusions and explain how the data gathered through your research will assist you. You should record…

- what you did
- why you did it
- what you hoped to find out (what your expectations were)

- what you actually found out
- how these findings will affect your design ideas.

You should use tables, charts and graphs where appropriate to present your findings clearly.

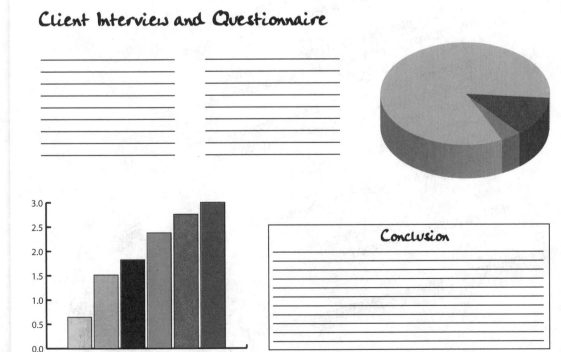

Client Interview and Questionnaire

Conclusion

Design Specification

Your design specification should provide a set of guidelines for your graphic product, based on…
- your analysis of the brief
- the findings of your research.

A design specification is often best displayed as a bullet point list.

You need to be clear about which criteria on the specification are essential and which are desirable, i.e. are not essential but would enhance the product.

You will need to refer to your specification when you start to generate and develop ideas to ensure that your designs are relevant and appropriate. That means it needs to be clear and specific and include information about…
- target market – who is the design aimed at?
  - Specify the age / age group and sex.
  - What is there occupation?
  - What are their interests?
  - Are there any handicaps, religious beliefs, differing attitudes and values that need to be considered?
  - Are their any socio-economic factors that need to be considered, e.g. single mothers?
- function – what is the purpose of your design?
- environment – where will the design be used?
- size – is there a specific size or size limit for your design?
- weight – is there a minimum or maximum weight for your design?
- durability – how long is the product expected to last?
- aesthetics – are there any restrictions on colour, shape, form, etc.?
- materials – does the product need to be waterproof, fireproof, easy to clean, lightweight, flexible, strong, etc.?
- cost – what is the budget?
- environmental issues – does the product need to be easy to dispose of or recycle? Does it need to be made from sustainable materials?
- manufacture – will the product be mass, batch, or one-off produced?
- packaging – does the product need to be packaged for retail?
- instructions – do instructions or aftercare guidelines need to be supplied with the product?

Initial Ideas

Generating ideas is an important part of any design process, and you should allow yourself plenty of time for this stage. This is your chance to show off your creative skills, but make sure your ideas…

- are realistic and workable
- address all the essential criteria on your design specification.

Your initial ideas are likely to take the form of rough sketches on paper.

Many people find this the hardest part of the design process, but don't panic if your mind goes blank! Here are some methods you could experiment with:

Drawing through a window – select an object of interest (nature is a good source) and focus on one part of it to produce interesting shapes and patterns.

In the style of… – borrow elements from past design movements, e.g. Bauhaus, Art Deco, Shaker.

Setting rules – set yourself rules, e.g. you can only use straight lines and two circles in your design.

Look at famous designers – look at the work of famous designers past and present for inspiration.

Look at current trends – look for trends in the designs of products similar to yours / intended for the same target market as yours that you can focus on.

Working with grids – use squared paper or cut-out symmetrical shapes and experiment with repeated patterns.

You need to present your initial ideas clearly, but remember there are no marks for 'pretty'.

To show how your design ideas relate to the criteria on your design specification, try using sketches with notes and annotations.

Don't worry about how good your drawings are at this stage; it is the variety and feasibility of the ideas that are important.

Reviewing Ideas

You need to review and evaluate your initial ideas to select one or two to develop further.

They must satisfy the essential criteria on your design specification, but you will also want to consider…

- which designs satisfy the most desirable criteria
- which designs are most unique / innovative
- which designs are most appealing / attractive
- which designs are most sustainable / environmentally friendly.

Ask your client / end-user for their opinion – which ones would they buy?

Developing Ideas

Development is another important part of the design process. Your aim at this stage is to modify and revise your initial idea(s) until you reach the best possible design solution.

When your teacher and the moderator look at your development sheets they will expect to see a design that is much improved compared to your initial idea.

To help you make the necessary modifications…

- use tests to ensure that your final design meets all the essential criteria on your design specification
- make models to test your ideas
- use ICT where appropriate, e.g. to experiment with different colourways
- continuously evaluate your designs against the design specification
- ask your client / end-user for feedback.

Once you feel that you have reached the best possible design solution, make sure it is presented in a way that someone else can understand. Provide clear diagrams that are fully annotated.

At this stage, you need to use your knowledge of a wide range of materials, components and manufacturing processes. Your work should show a good understanding of…

- properties of materials and / or components
- the advantages / disadvantages of materials and / or components
- the advantages / disadvantages of manufacturing processes.

This means you must select the most appropriate materials, components and manufacturing processes for your product and justify your choices.

At the end of this process you should have enough information to produce a detailed product specification and / or manufacturing specification.

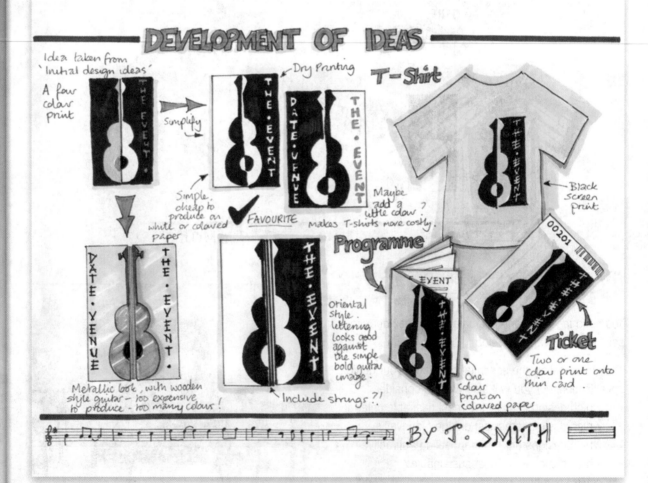

Using ICT

You should use of a range of communication techniques and media, including ICT and CAD, where appropriate throughout the design and make task(s). This is particularly important at the development stage.

This can include…

- standard applications, like Word or Excel
- specialist software, e.g. ProDesktop, 2D Design and Google SketchUp.
- digital camera
- scanner
- CAD / CAM.

Computer Aided Design (CAD) software keeps developing and improving. If it is available to you and it is appropriate, you should try to use some CAD for at least part of your final design.

You might use CAD to…

- make templates
- improve the accuracy and clarity of your drawings
- create numerical data for use on CNC machinery
- create 3D representations of your designs
- make and test scale models / prototypes.

It is vital to include a series of screen grabs in your project folder, so the moderator can see how you used CAD, the changes you made, and how it was used to set up any CAM equipment.

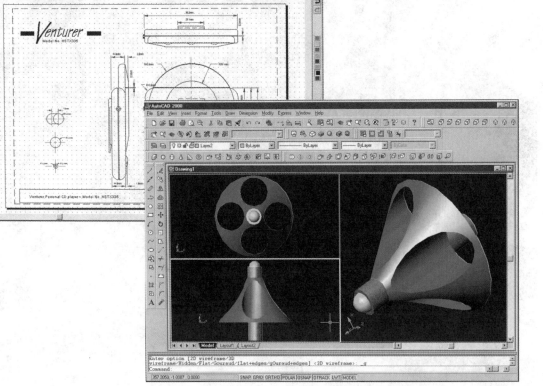

Modelling

Modelling (i.e. making models and / or mock-ups) is an essential part of the development process. It allows you to…

- check that your overall design works in practice
- experiment with a variety of suitable processes and techniques
- compare different methods of joining and finishing.

Depending on the size of your product, you may choose to produce full size models or scale models, e.g. 1:1, 1:2, 1:5, 1:10, etc.

Always use materials that are easy to work with, for example…

- block foam / Styrofoam™
- foam board
- plaster bandage
- board
- acrylic (plastic)
- medium density fibreboard (MDF)
- balsa wood
- hard wax
- corrugated plastic sheet.

Make sure you take the correct precautions and use cutting equipment safely.

Some computer programs can model your designs and enable you to view it from different angles. Sometimes this can take longer than sketching a model, however it does allow you to make modifications and changes without having to start from scratch each time.

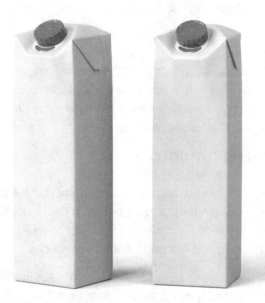

Product Specification

Your product specification will be more detailed and technical than your design specification. It should include...

- working drawings (drawn, sketched or CAD) – orthographic or isometric drawings, showing accurate dimensions
- assembly instructions
- a list of materials, colours and finishes
- a risk assessment (see below).

Your working drawing must follow basic industry standards, for example...

- use the correct type of line to show outlines or edges, projection or dimension lines and centre lines or lines of symmetry
- use millimeters to dimension drawings and write the number only
- position numbers above and in the middle of dimension lines
- include the scale on the drawing.

You should use your product specification to put together a production plan and build and test a prototype of your end product.prototype of your end product.

Risk Assessment

Look at each process in turn and make a list of possible health and safety risks.

Work back through the list and plan how your will minimise the risks, e.g. by wearing safety equipment, by ensuring you know how to use the tools correctly, etc.

Production Plan

Your production plan should show...

- the different stages of manufacture in the correct order
- when and what quality control checks will take place.

A flow chart might be the best way of presenting your production plan although sometimes a simple chart listing the stages and the equipment that will be used is equally suitable.

A Gantt chart can be used to show the timings for each stage of production and the overall timeline.

If you draw a flow chart, there are different, specific symbols for each stage of the process. Some are shown opposite.

The symbols are linked together by arrows to show the correct sequence of events.

You should aim to keep your flow chart as clear and simple as possible.

Flow Chart Symbols

Terminator
Represents start, restart and stop.

Process
Represents a particular instruction or action.

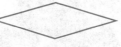

Decision
Represents a choice that can lead to another pathway.

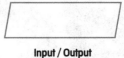

Input / Output
Represents additions to / removals from a particular process.

Flow Chart

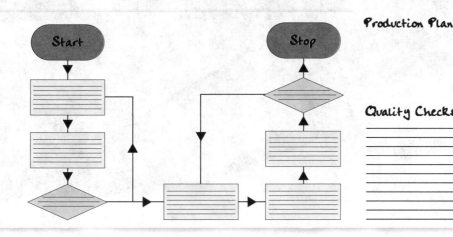

Manufacture

In making the prototype of your final product you should demonstrate that, for each specific task, you can select and use…

- appropriate tools and equipment
- appropriate processes, methods and techniques (including CAD / CAM where relevant)
- appropriate materials
- appropriate quality control checks.

You can do this by carrying out the necessary practical processes correctly and safely and with precision and accuracy.

Remember, all the materials, methods and processes that you choose must help to make your product the best possible design solution for the brief. Don't include something just to show off your skills!

The finished product should be…

- accurately assembled
- well finished
- fully functional.

Don't worry if it doesn't turn out quite the way you hoped though – you will earn marks for all the skills and processes you demonstrate, so make sure you record them all clearly in your folder.

*For each stage of production, you might want to include…

- a list and / or photograph of materials used
- a list and / or photograph of tools used
- a flow chart / step-by-step description of the process carried out
- an explanation of any safety measures you had to take.

N.B. There are no marks available from AQA for doing this.

Industry

You should have a good understanding of the methods and processes used in graphic design and manufacturing industries.

Although you will probably only produce one final product, it is important to show that you are aware of various possible methods of production and how your product would be manufactured commercially. You should explain this in your project folder.

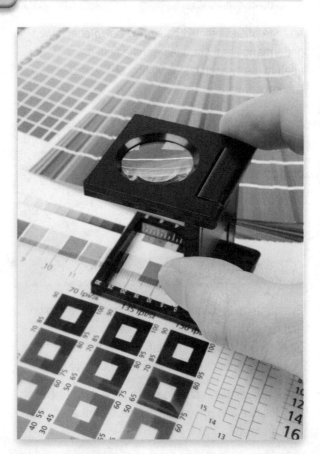

If your product could potentially be manufactured using several different methods, try to list the pros and cons for each method and then use these lists to make a decision about which method you would recommend.

If you know that a method or process you are using to make your product would be carried out differently in a factory, make a note of this in your project folder – this will show your teacher and moderator how much you know!

Testing

A range of tests should be carried out to check the performance and / or quality of the final product. You need to justify each test you carry out, i.e. explain why it is important.

Tests do not have to be complicated. They just need to be sensible and helpful, e.g. test that the product meets with the criteria on your design and / or product specifications.

Keeping records is very important. In your project folder you need to…

- explain what tests were carried out
- explain why the tests were carried out
- describe what you found out
- explain what modifications you would make based on the test results
- include a photo of the prototype in use.

You should not test your prototype to destruction, but it is a good idea to take photos of your product before testing begins just in case anything goes wrong.

Evaluation

Evaluation is an ongoing process. During the design and development process, every decision you made (providing it is clearly justified) and all the client / end-user feedback counts towards your evaluation.

The final evaluation should summarise all your earlier conclusions and provide an objective evaluation of the final prototype.

When carrying out an evaluation, you should…

- refer back to the brief
- cross-check the end product against the original specification
- obtain client comments and feedback
- take a photograph of the client using the product
- carry out a simple end-user survey.

You need to establish…

- whether the product meets all the criteria on the original brief and specification
- whether the product is easy to use
- whether the product functions the way it was intended to
- what consumers think of the style of the product
- whether consumers like / dislike any features
- whether consumers would purchase the product and what they would be prepared to pay for it
- what consumers think the advantages and disadvantages are compared to similar products
- what impact making and using the product has on the environment.

Depending on what you find out, you can include suggestions for further modifications in your evaluation.

Honesty is the best policy when writing evaluations. If something didn't work, say so – but always suggest a way of preventing the same problem from occurring in the future.

Blow Moulding

The **blow moulding** process is the same as the extrusion process, but an air supply and split mould is used instead of the cooling chamber.

Common materials used are...

- polyvinyl chloride
- polyethylene
- polypropylene.

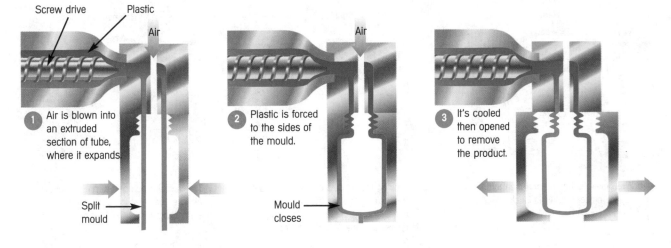

Screw drive   Plastic

Air

1. Air is blown into an extruded section of tube, where it expands.

Split mould

Air

2. Plastic is forced to the sides of the mould.

Mould closes

3. It's cooled then opened to remove the product.

Compression Moulding

Compression moulding is a process where a hydraulic press applies a downward force to create a shape from a heated piece of plastic.

Common materials used are...

- phenol
- urea formaldehyde and melamine formaldehyde.

A large force is used to squash a cube of polymer into a heated mould. This cube of polymer is in the form of a powder, known as a 'slug'. Compression moulding is used with thermosetting plastics.

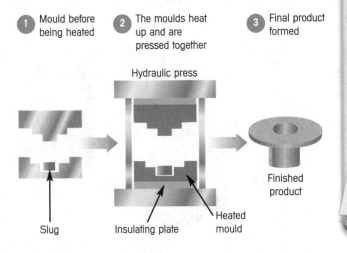

1. Mould before being heated
2. The moulds heat up and are pressed together
3. Final product formed

Hydraulic press

Slug   Insulating plate   Heated mould

Finished product

Industrial Processes

Vacuum Forming

Vacuum forming is where a sheet of plastic is heated up and pressed against a mould to produce an impression of that shape. You can use this technique at school to make models.

Vacuum forming uses thermoplastic materials in the form of sheets which can measure up to 1.5m x 1.8m. The most popular material is **polystyrene** (styrene) which is cheap and easy to form.

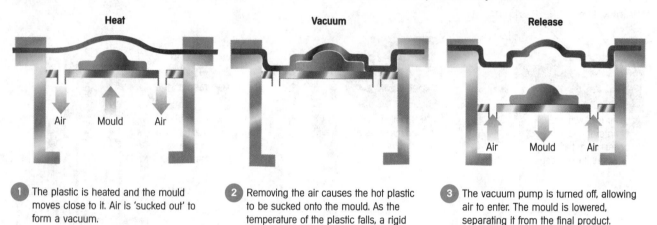

1. The plastic is heated and the mould moves close to it. Air is 'sucked out' to form a vacuum.

2. Removing the air causes the hot plastic to be sucked onto the mould. As the temperature of the plastic falls, a rigid impression of the mould is formed.

3. The vacuum pump is turned off, allowing air to enter. The mould is lowered, separating it from the final product.

Line Bending

Acrylic sheets are often bent using a **line bending** machine or strip heater:

1. The plastic sheet is heated along the line of the intended fold by a special heating element.

2. Temperature switches control the amount of heat produced to cater for different thicknesses of material.

3. The softened area is bent into shape using a **bending jig** to achieve the right shape and angle.

It's important that you keep your fingers away from the heat element of a line bending machine and always remember to switch it off after use.

Line Bending Machine

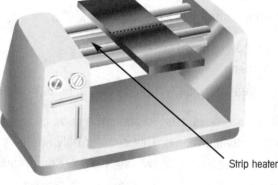

Strip heater

Bending Jig

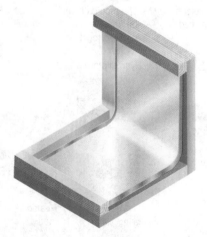

Laser Cutting

Laser cutting is a process where a piece of material is cut using a **laser beam** – a powerful wattage laser beam produced inside the machine.

A series of **mirrors** direct the laser beam vertically down onto the material to be cut (called 'flying optics').

As the laser beam hits the material, the intense heat vapourises it – leaving a polished face.

Motorised actuators move the mirrors to adjust the cutting position while the laser supply remains stationary.

The materials that can be cut using lasers are…
- acrylic, acetate and several other plastics
- paper, card and wood
- leather and suede
- many different fabrics from silk to denim
- sign making materials including self-adhesive films, reflective and retro-reflective materials
- laser cut polyester / metal sheeting for stencils.

Laser Cutting Machine

Laser Cutter Cutting a Plate of Steel

Quick Test

1. What types of material does vacuum forming use?
2. What is sucked out to form a vacuum so the plastic takes the shape of the mould?
3. A laser beam is directed vertically down onto the material by what?
4. What is the importance of a jig?
5. Which type of plastic is commonly used for line bending?

KEY WORDS
Make sure you understand these words before moving on!
- Vacuum forming
- Line bending
- Bending jig
- Laser cutting

Industrial Practice

Methods of Production

Logistics is ensuring that the **right materials and resources** are in the **right place** at the **right time**, in order to maximise the efficiency of the manufacturing process.

Although you will only manufacture one final product from your design, it's important that you are aware of the various possible methods of production and how yours could be produced commercially.

Cell production is the production of **individual parts** of a product, which are made independently (**known as cells**). Then at the end of a manufacturing cycle, all the individual parts are assembled to make one product. For example, a car or a mobile phone.

One-off production is when one product is made at one particular time, sometimes known as a **prototype**. It can take a long time and be expensive. An example is a display for an exhibition stand.

Batch production is a series of products that are made together in either small or large quantities.

Mass production / repetitive flow involves the product being produced for days or even weeks and in large numbers resulting in the product being relatively inexpensive. A typical product could be a fancy chocolate box or car assembly.

Continuous production is where a product is continually produced over a period of hours, days or even years. This sort of production very often results in the product being relatively inexpensive, e.g. a milk carton.

Just in Time Production (JIT) involves the arrival of component parts at exactly the time they are needed at the factory. This allows for less storage space, saving on costly warehousing. But, if the supply of components is stopped, the production line stops, which then becomes very costly.

Printing

Printing has been used for many years to produce graphic products. There are many factors to take into consideration when choosing the right method of printing your product. Your choice of which method to use is determined by the cost, quality and quantity required.

Methods of Printing

Relief printing is a method in which inked wood, lino or metal has paper pressed onto it to produce a print. The most common types are **letterpressing** and **block printing**.

Letterpress prints from a **raised surface**:
- This surface receives ink and is then pressed onto the paper.
- This process is expensive as metal letters have to be individually made.
- Letterpress is now only used for high-quality books and stationery, generally in short runs.

In **block printing** the image is **drawn onto lino**, then the lino is cut away from around the image so the image sits proud of the surface. Ink is applied, then the paper is pressed onto the lino using a roller, so the image is transferred onto the paper.

Flexography is similar to the letterpress process, but instead of using flat printing plates, it uses flexible rubber or plastic plates for **cylinders**.
- The cylinders rotate to print onto paper, card, plastic or metal.
- Flexography is used for packaging, cartons or point of sale material.

Letterpress

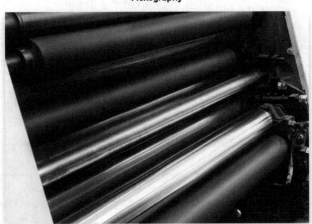

Flexography

Quick Test

1. Name a product that can be produced as a one-off.
2. Name a product produced by continuous production.
3. What are the most common types of relief printing?
4. Why is the letterpress an expensive printing process?
5. What is the difference between flexography and letterpress printing?

KEY WORDS
Make sure you understand these words before moving on!
- Logistics
- Cell production
- One-off production
- Continuous production
- Relief printing
- Letterpress
- Block printing
- Flexography

Printing Processes

Gravure Printing

The **gravure** process is used when producing **high-quality prints in large volumes** (e.g. 500 000– 1 000 000) as it's very expensive to set up. Gravure is used for high-quality reproduction of photos, paintings, full-colour magazines and books.

The gravure plate is made photographically:

1. Images are etched onto a plate through a screen. The image is broken down into dots.
2. Ink fills the **'dot' cells** and excess ink is removed using a 'doctor' blade.
3. Rubber-covered cylinders press the paper into the cell holes, creating a printed image. The deeper the holes, the darker the image.

Screen Printing

Screen printing can print designs onto T-shirts, bags, banners, signs, shopping bags, posters, packaging and flyers. Simple **stencils** can be made and used to produce relatively cheap prints fast and effectively.

More sophisticated commercial presses can produce thousands of copies per hour and produce a good thickness of ink on almost all surfaces.

The process goes through six stages:

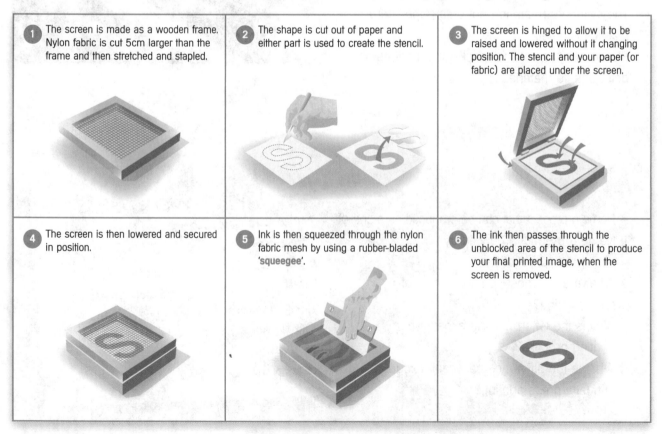

1. The screen is made as a wooden frame. Nylon fabric is cut 5cm larger than the frame and then stretched and stapled.

2. The shape is cut out of paper and either part is used to create the stencil.

3. The screen is hinged to allow it to be raised and lowered without it changing position. The stencil and your paper (or fabric) are placed under the screen.

4. The screen is then lowered and secured in position.

5. Ink is then squeezed through the nylon fabric mesh by using a rubber-bladed 'squeegee'.

6. The ink then passes through the unblocked area of the stencil to produce your final printed image, when the screen is removed.

Planographic Printing

The most common form of planographic printing is offset lithography, which is mainly used for commercial printing. This method works on the principle that water and grease don't mix. The image **attracts grease** (the ink) and **rejects water**. The areas which aren't being printed on reject the grease and attract water. The high speed and cheapness of the process makes it the most widely used method.

The best offset litho machines will print in 'full colour' on both sides of the paper in one go:

- They rely on a **four colour process** using **cyan** (a shade of blue), **magenta** (a shade of red), **yellow** and **black**, known as the CMYK process.
- Black is applied last, as it creates tone.
- Filters are responsible for the **colour separation** and a screen converts the separate colours into individual dots, which form the final image.

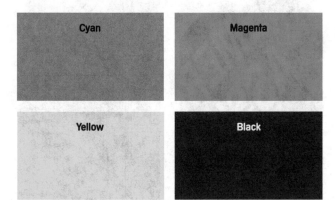

The process has a **printing plate**, with the image in relief which is free to rotate. Ink is applied to the printing plate, which is dampened. This repels ink off any non-image areas. The printing plate then transfers an inked image onto the **rubber blanket cylinder**, which in turn presses the image onto the paper or card as it's fed through.

Small machines often use disposable paper printing plates to print letterheads, business cards and leaflets, in one or two print runs, of up to 5000 copies.

A medium run for larger machines prints between 5000 and 20 000 copies.

Web-fed machines run from a **continuous roll of paper** which is cheaper than pre-cut paper. But, it takes a long time to set the machines up, so is only economical for large print runs.

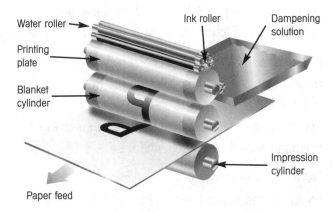

Quick Test

1. How is the gravure plate made?
2. What is the image broken up into on the gravure plate?
3. What tool is used to squeeze ink through nylon fabric in screen printing?
4. In screen printing, what do you need to create from paper first?
5. What does CMYK stand for?

KEY WORDS
Make sure you understand these words before moving on!
- Gravure
- Screen printing
- Stencils
- Squeegee
- Offset lithography
- CMYK
- Tone

Printing Processes

Dry Printing

The general name given to the dry printing process, used by photocopiers and laser printers, is **xerography**.

Photocopiers are used for taking copies from books, laser prints and photographs. They can enlarge and reduce images.

Laser printers are used for one-off development work and can print work from computer aided design packages. These packages print on a 'WYSIWYG' principle, which stands for '**What You See Is What You Get**'. In other words, they will print exactly what you see on your screen.

Finishes

There are many different finishes that can be applied to printed products to improve their look and design.

Embossing raises or indents selected areas of a design, e.g. lettering or a pattern.

Hot-foil blocking is when you emboss an image onto foil.

Holographic printing produces a pattern that, although flat, appears to have **three dimensions**. Layers of metallic foil are used to achieve this effect.

Microencapsulation is a process by which microcapsules are formed. When the microcapsules burst, tiny particles are released. For example, scratch-and-sniff stickers use microcapsules that **release a scent** when scratched.

UV varnishing is a high-gloss varnish (a clear liquid) that is applied over the top of a printed area to produce a **glossy finish.**

Varnish can be applied to specific areas to highlight features of a design (spot varnishing) or to the entire surface.

Lamination uses heat to apply a layer of protective, **transparent film** to the surface of a printed image. This process is often used on book covers.

Embossing (Braille)   Holographic

Book Binding
Edexcel

Saddle wire stitching is where pages are **stitched** through the **fold line** at the spine. Magazines or catalogues use this method. It's ideal for projects with no more than 60 to 80 pages and is the simplest and most economical way to bind.

Perfect binding is where pages are **assembled in groups**, or signatures, and bound together with flexible **adhesive**, then covered with a hard back cover. Paper back books and catalogues use this binding method.

Hard binding uses a **rigid cover** and **stitching** in the spine of the book. The covers of modern hard back books are made of thick cardboard or clothette.

Comb binding uses a 9/16" pitch rectangular hole pattern punched near the bound edge. A **curled plastic 'comb'** is fed through slits, which holds the sheets together. This allows a book to be taken apart and put back together again by hand without damage.

Planning Your Work

There are various ways of planning your work so that you can design and make to schedule.

A **Gantt chart** helps to break down all the tasks you have to complete into segments.

Process	Time Involved (mins)			
	5	10	15	20
Sew centre front seam				
Sew centre back seam				
Sew outer left seam				
Sew outer right seam				
Check seam allowances				
Sew inner leg seam				
Create drawstring channel				
Insert drawstring				
Hem legs				

A **flow chart** shows the order in which a series of tasks is carried out. Different shaped boxes represent the various stages that need to be carried out when planning your work:

- TERMINATOR ( ) – the 'start' and the 'end' of a process.
- DECISION ◇ – shows that a choice needs to be made about what to do next.
- PROCESS ▭ – a particular instruction or action.
- INPUT / OUTPUT ▱ – shows things that need to be added or taken away from the process.

Flow Chart Identifying the Basic Process of Making Several Copies Using a Photocopier.

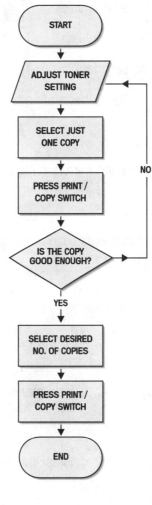

Plan of Manufacture

A plan of manufacture provides details of the resources needed and the sequence of tasks that need to be completed to make a product. You need to include…

- materials needed
- dimensions
- tools needed
- a list of tasks / processes (as a flow chart or written schedule)
- time required for each stage
- a risk assessment
- details of quality control checks
- diagrams of each stage.

KEY WORDS

Make sure you understand these words before moving on!

- Xerography
- WYSIWYG
- Embossing
- Holographic
- Gantt chart
- Flow chart

Practice Questions

1. In which manufacturing process would a sheet of plastic get heated up and pressed against a mould to produce an impression of that shape? Tick the correct option.

   A Extrusion

   B Injection moulding

   C Blow moulding

   D Vacuum forming

2. How are acrylic sheets often bent?

3. What moves the mirrors on a laser cutting machine to adjust the cutting position?

4. List three materials used in compression moulding.

   a)

   b)

   c)

5. What are thermochromic materials made of?

6. **a)** What are phosphorescent materials also known as?

   b) How can phosphorescent be applied to materials?

7. Name the manufacturing process shown in the diagram below.

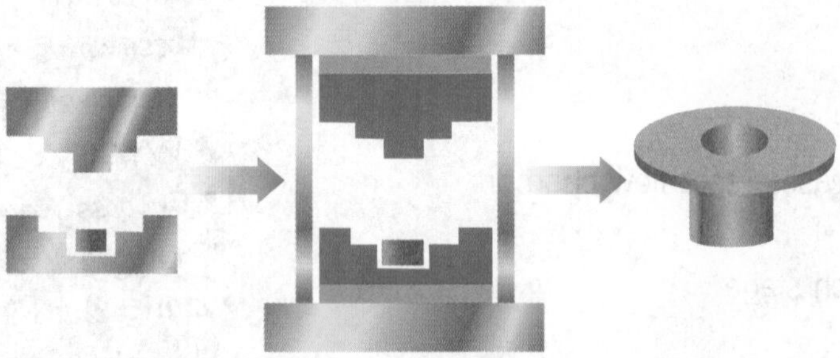

8 List three health and safety rules you need to follow when using paints and inks.

a) ....

b) ....

c) ....

9 a) What are eyelets also known as?

....

b) How many parts do eyelets come in?

....

c) How are these parts put together?

....

10 Describe double-sided tape.

....

....

11 Explain why a safety ruler is safer than a normal ruler.

....

12 What do you do when masking fluid dries?

....

13 What is the hand-held version of a scroll saw called?

....

14 The diagram below shows letters of the alphabet in braille.

What is the process called that indents or raises this pattern? ....

Packaging and Mechanisms

Developments

A surface **development** or **net** is a two dimensional shape which when scored, folded and glued together forms a three-dimensional package, carton or container.

It is important that…
- all the adjacent edges are equal, so that when they are folded together they are the same length
- the print is the right way up when assembled.

In industry, developments are arranged on a sheet with minimal gaps between them (called a **tessellation pattern**) in order to minimise waste.

Die cutters are used to press out the shape of the development while **creasing bars** are used to create the folds in the development.

You can produce and manipulate surface developments using a CAD software system.

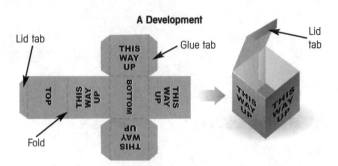

A Development

Lid tab · Glue tab · Lid tab · TOP · THIS WAY UP · BOTTOM · THIS WAY UP · THIS WAY UP · Fold

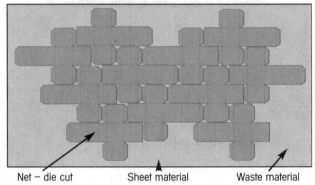

Tessellation Pattern for Series of Developments

Net – die cut · Sheet material · Waste material

'Tuck In'

'Tuck in'…
- is the **tab** on the end of the lid, which **holds the lid closed**
- when made commercially often has rounded corners to smooth out the closing
- has short slits to help 'lock' the lid in place.

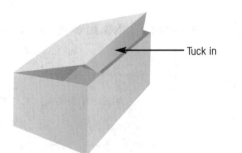

Tuck in

Automatic Bases

Automatic bases (crash lock)…
- is a **net of a box**, that has an automatic base
- is a box assembled **flat packed**, so when it needs to be used, you open up the box by pushing out the base.

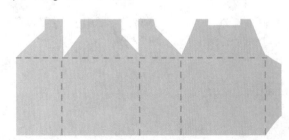

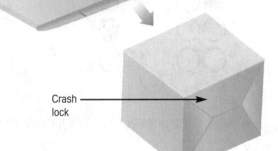

Crash lock

Functions of Packaging

Packaging is big business and one that we often take for granted. It has four main objectives.

Objective	Reason	
Preserve	• Food products are packed to keep them fresh for longer • To ensure that products are sold hygienically and conveniently	
Protect	• To make sure that the contents of the goods arrive at the shops and at home without damage or contamination • To reduce theft of parts	
Promote / inform	• Labels provide information about a product, e.g. the contents, weight and how it can be used • Labels are also used as a sales and marketing tool	
Transport	• Goods are packaged into crates or cartons, often called 'outers', so that they can be handled, stacked and transported quickly and efficiently, without fear of breakage	

Quick Test

1. Name four functions of packaging.
2. What is the other word for a surface development?
3. What is the other word for an automatic base?
4. When developments are arranged on a sheet with minimal waste, what is this called?
5. What are goods packed into to be transported?

KEY WORDS

Make sure you understand these words before moving on!

- Development
- 'Tuck in'
- Automatic bases
- Preserve
- Protect
- Promote/inform
- Transport

Packaging Materials

Paper and Board Packaging

Paper and board packaging is made from wood pulp and waste paper. Board is made to a much thicker and heavier specification than paper. Paper is used mainly for paper bags and labels.

Corrugated cardboard is used in packaging and formed from **layers** of **paper** which can be made into boxes for packing electrical goods, books, etc. The **'wavy'** layer in corrugated cardboard is called **'fluting'**, which is designed to **absorb** any impact during **transportation**.

Folding boxboard can be single or multi-ply, coated or uncoated. It has good folding properties, stiffness and scoring ability.

Spiral bound tubes are made from long lengths of cardboard, laminated into a tube. They are used for toilet / kitchen rolls, and for the transportation and packaging of goods.

Paper and board can be used together with layers of thin **aluminium foil** or **plastic** to form a **lamination**. **Foil-lined board** is commonly used for ready made meals or take away meals.

The foil retains heat, keeping food warm. Foil lamination is also used in drink cartons, yoghurt pot lids, crisp packets and confectionary.

Tetra Pak™ is a brand name for a carton that preserves and packages drinks.

Advantages of Paper and Board

The **advantages** of paper and board packaging are that...
* the materials are **light weight**
* they are **easy to handle** and store
* they are **easy to fold** and crease
* when **laminated** with foil or plastic, a seal can be created to prevent evaporation and to preserve the product
* the **colour printing** can be produced to a high quality
* they are **environmentally friendly**, since they can be recycled.

Computer disc packaging are examples of products that can be recycled and produced flat-packed.

Plastic Packaging

The following are the most common types of plastic packaging.

Polyvinyl chloride (PVC) is used for…
- bottles which contain shampoo and juice
- blister packs for DIY products.

High density polyethylene (HDPE) is used for…
- detergent, milk and fruit juice bottles
- bottle caps
- frozen food packaging.

Low density polyethylene (LDPE) is used for…
- bin liners and bags
- squeezy bottles
- frozen food packaging.

Polystyrene (PS) is used for…
- egg cartons
- yoghurt pots
- food trays.

Polypropylene (PP) is used for…
- squeezy bottles for sauce (as it's very robust)
- bottle caps
- film packs for biscuits and crisps.

Polyethylene terephthalate (PET) is used for…
- fizzy drink bottles (as it's stiff and tough)
- oven ready meal roasting bags.

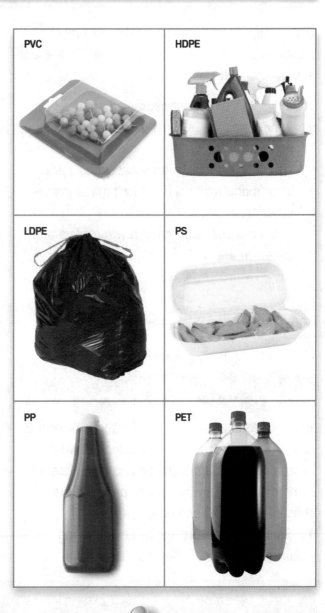

Quick Test

1. When used for packaging what is paper mainly useful for?
2. What is the wavy section in corrugated cardboard known as?
3. What does HDPE stand for?
4. Name two pieces of HDPE packaging.
5. What is used in drink cartons, yoghurt pot lids, crisp packets and confectionary?

KEY WORDS

Make sure you understand these words before moving on!

- Corrugated cardboard
- Fluting
- Lamination
- PVC
- HDPE
- LDPE
- PS
- PP
- PET

Packaging Materials

Glass Packaging

Glass is made from natural, sustainable raw materials and is used for bottle and jars in the food and beverage industry.

The advantages of glass packaging are that…
- it maintains the purity of food and preserves the taste
- it's 100% recyclable in a closed loop system
- it's a mono-material (i.e. it isn't made from other materials)
- it reduces consumption of raw materials and saves on energy.

Which Packaging to Use?

You need to analyse existing packaging in order to create new designs. You need to look at what packaging suits what purpose and why. Here are some examples of why specific packaging is chosen for specific products:
- Some products are affected by **light and oxygen**, e.g. oils, coffee and fat.
- Some foods are affected by **moisture**, e.g. meat and biscuits.
- Some drinks can absorb **smells and taste**, e.g. mineral water and milk.

The table shows the advantages, disadvantages and uses of various types of packaging.

Material	Advantages	Disadvantages	Uses
Paper and card	• Low density • Low cost	• Affected by water / moisture	• Toys • Cereals • Washing powders
Plastic (thermoplastic)	• Low density • Waterproof • Can be reheated	• Affected by heat	• Drinks • Shampoos
Metal, e.g. steel, aluminium	• Strong • Waterproof	• Expensive • High density	• Tinned food • Fizzy drinks
Glass	• Waterproof • Transparent	• Shatters • Expensive • High density	• More expensive drinks • Coffee

Types of Movement   AQA • OCR

A mechanism creates **movement** within a product. Mechanisms in graphic products are used to provide movement in display models, pop-up cards and other products with moving parts, e.g. a moving sign or a board game.

There are four types of movement:

- **rotating**
- **linear**
- **reciprocating**
- **oscillating**.

The following pages give you a basic understanding of how mechanisms work. This will help you when you begin to develop your design ideas.

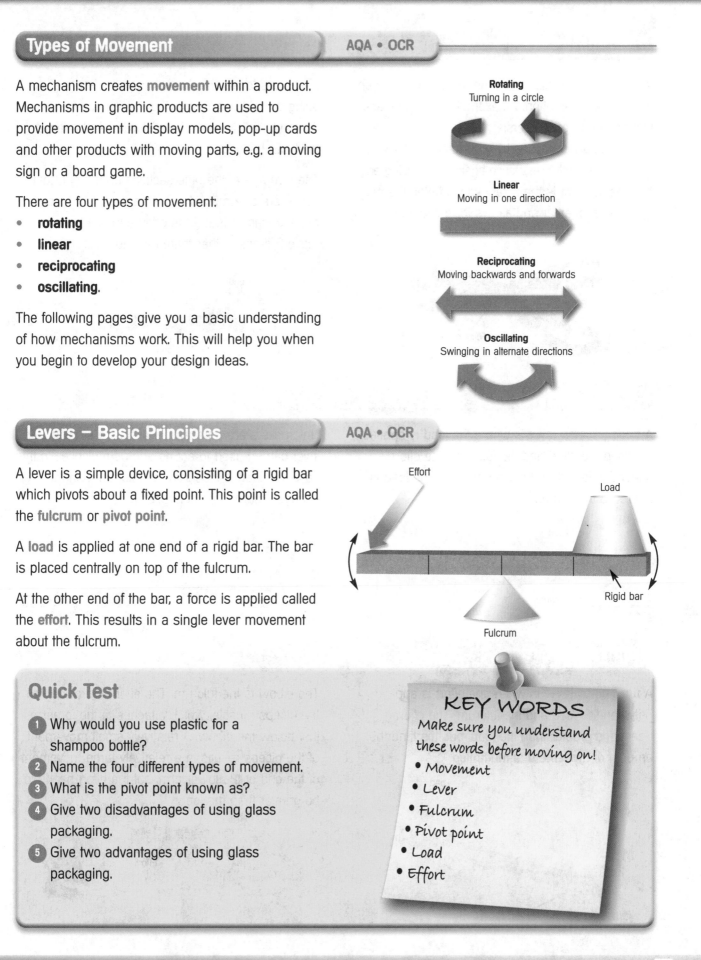

Rotating
Turning in a circle

Linear
Moving in one direction

Reciprocating
Moving backwards and forwards

Oscillating
Swinging in alternate directions

Levers – Basic Principles   AQA • OCR

A lever is a simple device, consisting of a rigid bar which pivots about a fixed point. This point is called the **fulcrum** or **pivot point**.

A **load** is applied at one end of a rigid bar. The bar is placed centrally on top of the fulcrum.

At the other end of the bar, a force is applied called the **effort**. This results in a single lever movement about the fulcrum.

Effort

Load

Rigid bar

Fulcrum

Quick Test

1. Why would you use plastic for a shampoo bottle?
2. Name the four different types of movement.
3. What is the pivot point known as?
4. Give two disadvantages of using glass packaging.
5. Give two advantages of using glass packaging.

KEY WORDS

Make sure you understand these words before moving on!

- Movement
- Lever
- Fulcrum
- Pivot point
- Load
- Effort

Types of Movement

First Class Levers

A **first class lever** is where the fulcrum is between the load and the effort. An example of a first class lever is a pair of scissors:

- The **effort** is applied by your hand at one end.
- The **load** is the resistance against the cutting edge.
- The **fulcrum** is the screw which holds the two halves together and allows for movement.

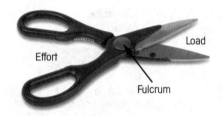

First class levers can be **force multipliers**, e.g. using a crow bar. By moving the fulcrum nearer to the load, the effort can be multiplied and a larger load can be lifted.

The leverage of the blue sections on the rigid bar below are at a ratio of 1:3, so an effort of 1 could move a load of 3, but the effort end will have to move 3 times further than the load end.

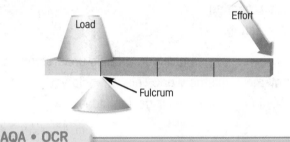

Second Class Levers

A **second class lever** is where the load is applied between the effort and the fulcrum. The effort needed is less than the load because the load is nearer to the fulcrum.

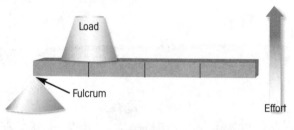

Nutcrackers are an example of how a second class lever can be used to act as a force multiplier. In this case, the load is closer to the fulcrum than the effort, so more force is applied.

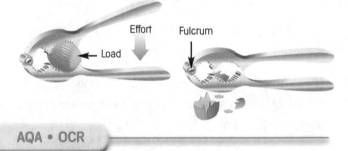

Third Class Levers

A **third class lever** is where the effort is applied between the load and the fulcrum. The effort needed is greater than the load, but this time the amount of **movement is multiplied**.

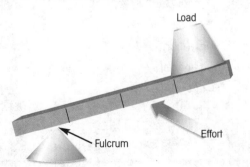

The elbow is the fulcrum. The effort is provided by the biceps muscle, which attaches to the forearm just below the elbow. A relatively small movement of the biceps results in a relatively large movement of the end of the lower arm, but the effort needs to be greater than the load.

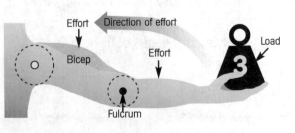

Cranks
AQA • OCR

Cranks are relatively simple devices that convert **rotary motion** to **linear motion**.

For example, as the pedals on a tricycle are moved around, the tricycle moves forwards.

Rotary motion ➡ Linear motion

Cams
AQA • OCR

A **cam** is a device that converts one type of movement into another.

For example, a **rotary cam** converts **rotary motion** into **reciprocating motion** (up and down movement) in the cam follower. This motion can be varied by using different shaped cams.

A **follower** is a rod that moves up and down. This will have an object of your choice on top. A **guide** holds the follower in place.

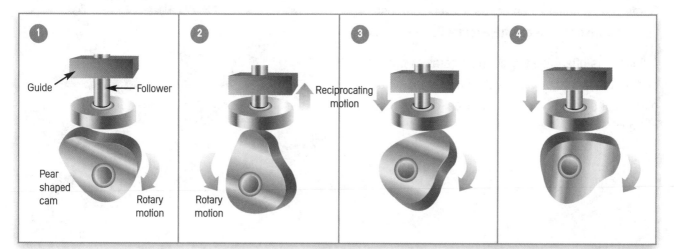

1. Guide — Follower — Pear shaped cam — Rotary motion
2. Rotary motion
3. Reciprocating motion
4.

Quick Test

1. A nutcracker is an example of which type of lever?
2. What type of muscle in the body is a movement multiplier?
3. What type of movement can cranks convert rotary movement to?
4. A follower moves in which direction?

KEY WORDS
Make sure you understand these words before moving on!
- First class lever
- Force multiplier
- Second class lever
- Third class lever
- Cranks
- Linear motion
- Cams

Types of Movement

Springs
AQA • OCR

There are many different types of spring that are used in a variety of ways to resist different forces.

They can be placed into **four** broad groups:
- Springs that resist **extension**.
- Springs that resist **compression**.
- Springs that resist **radial movement**.
- Springs that resist **twisting**.

These types of springs are normally used in resistant materials but the same principles can be applied in graphic products by using certain types of modern plastics.

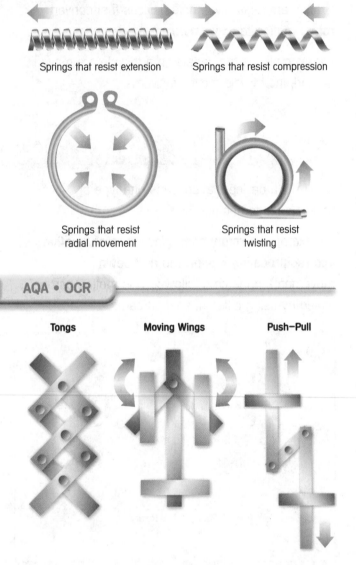

Springs that resist extension

Springs that resist compression

Springs that resist radial movement

Springs that resist twisting

Linkages
AQA • OCR

Sometimes a linkage can act as a lever, but most times it **transfers one mechanical motion to another**.

A linkage is often used to connect cams to cranks or cams to levers or vice versa. An example is a metal tool box which opens to reveal different levels of trays.

Tongs **Moving Wings** **Push–Pull**

Gears
AQA • OCR

Gears are like linkages, **transferring one motion to another**. Gear wheels have teeth that mesh with the teeth of another gear.

Gears are used as force multipliers or reducers to make things go **faster or slower**. They are used on bikes, cars, hand whisks, salad spinners, toys and bottle openers.

In graphic products, gears can be used in 3D working models.

Chain and Sprocket
AQA • OCR

A bicycle chain uses a chain and sprocket to connect the pedals to the back wheel. As the pedal is pushed, the chain links with the sprocket and turns the wheel.

Sprockets make it possible to pedal comfortably up hill.

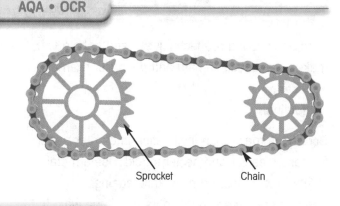

Sprocket   Chain

Pulley
AQA • OCR

A **pulley** is a **grooved wheel** with a belt running in the groove. A belt stretches, allowing it to absorb shock and be changed easily.

Pulleys are used to…
- **control how fast something turns**, e.g. cassette recorders and washing machines
- **make lifting things easier**, e.g. cranes.

The big wheel rotates more slowly than the small wheel, but with greater force.

A **twist** in the belt makes the wheels turn in the **opposite direction**.

In graphic products, pulleys can be used in 3D working models.

A Pulley

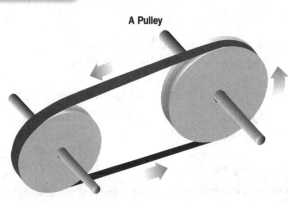

A Pulley with a Twist

Quick Test

1. List the four main types of spring.
2. Fill in the missing word.
   Gears are linkages for transferring ....
3. Give two uses of pulleys.
4. What does a twist in the belt of a pulley do?
5. What are gears and pulleys used for in graphic products?

KEY WORDS
Make sure you understand these words before moving on!
- Extension
- Compression
- Radial movement
- Linkage
- Gears
- Pulley

Mechanisms

Card Engineering   AQA • OCR

Card engineering are techniques used to help you make 3D products in card and paper, for example…

- **scoring**
- **folding**.

Scoring is making an indentation in card or paper to make it easier and neater to fold. Use a metal safety ruler to score a blunt knife against. Remember to keep your fingers out of the way. To create a **neat fold** after scoring, hold the metal ruler against the fold.

Another way to create a fold is to use a **creasing bar**. This retains the strength of the material.

Card and paper can be used for mechanisms for greetings cards, packaging and POS (Point-of-sale displays).

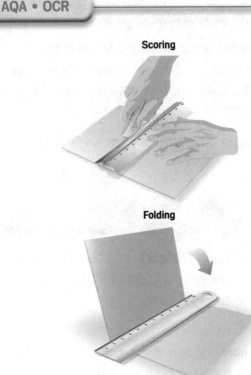

Scoring

Folding

V Fold Mechanism   AQA • OCR

A **V fold** is a simple fold. Glue is applied underneath the tabs. The centre of the V is lined up with the fold of the card. You can alter the angle of the V fold:

- At 90° the card will stand up when opened.
- At 60° the card will lean backwards when opened.
- At 100° the card will lean forwards when opened.

Glue tabs

Fold

Rotary Mechanism   AQA • OCR

A **rotary mechanism** gives a circular or rotating motion and works in the following way:

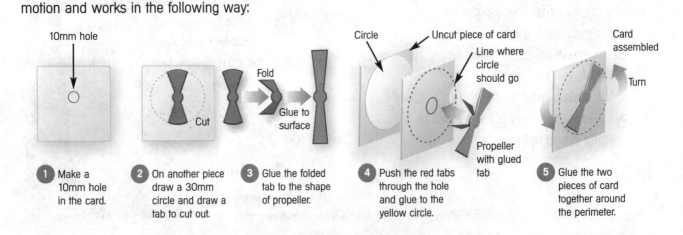

10mm hole

Fold

Cut

Glue to surface

Circle

Uncut piece of card

Line where circle should go

Propeller with glued tab

Card assembled

Turn

1. Make a 10mm hole in the card.
2. On another piece draw a 30mm circle and draw a tab to cut out.
3. Glue the folded tab to the shape of propeller.
4. Push the red tabs through the hole and glue to the yellow circle.
5. Glue the two pieces of card together around the perimeter.

Incised Mechanisms
AQA • OCR

An **incised mechanism** projects **one picture** out when the card opens. To make this you only need to do score lines from one piece of card. The lines should be parallel and the fold line should be in the centre. By moving the fold line, you can create a different shape.

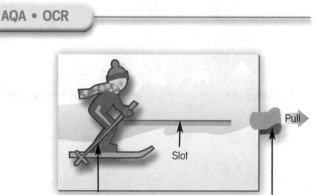

Score line

Fold line

Sliding Mechanisms
AQA • OCR

A **sliding mechanism** enables you to **move an image** in a single line, by pulling the end of a strip of card.

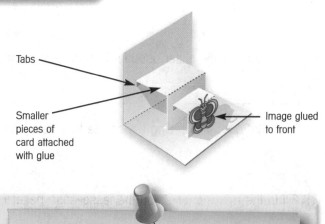

Pull

Slot

Image glued to small pieces of card

Strip of card attached to back

Layer Mechanisms
AQA • OCR

A **layer mechanism** enables you to put **images** on at **different levels** to the background, creating a 'layered' 3D image. It achieves the same objective as the incised mechanism but the projected images are made separately to the main piece of card and attached with glue. You can also glue images to the front.

Tabs

Smaller pieces of card attached with glue

Image glued to front

Quick Test

1. What two tools do you need to score card?
2. What angle does a V fold need to be set at for the card to stand up?
3. What type of mechanism would you use to create a spinning motion?
4. Where should the fold line be in incised mechanisms?

KEY WORDS
Make sure you understand these words before moving on!
- Scoring
- Creasing bar
- V fold
- Rotary mechanism
- Incised mechanism
- Sliding mechanism
- Layer mechanism

1 What does POS stand for?

_____

2 Name the three different types of card mechanisms below:

a)   **b)**    **c)**

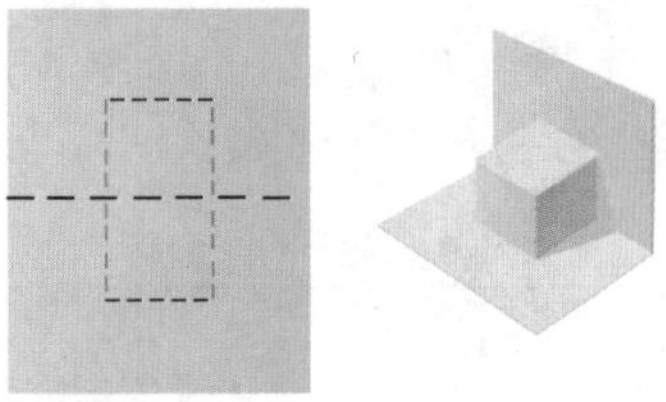

3 Explain the two methods you can use to fold card, when making card mechanisms.

a) _____

b) _____

4 Explain what a net is.

_____

_____

5 **a)**   What is a die cutter used for in a development?

_____

b)   What does a creasing bar create in a development?

_____

6 Fill in the missing labels on the tessellation pattern below.

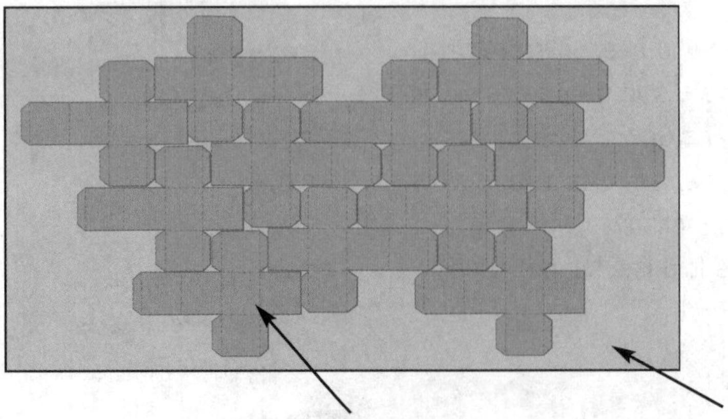

a) _____   **b)** _____

7 What is a 'tuck-in' tab?

....

8 What is the material that has a fluted centre also known as?

....

9 What is PVC generally used to make?

....

10 What does LDPE stand for?

....

11 List three factors that products need to be protected from.

a) ....

b) ....

c) ....

12 a) What are pulleys used to control?

....

b) Give an example of one.

....

13 What is the purpose of gears?

....

14 What is the motion a circular cam's follower makes?

....

15 In mechanical movement, what is the applied force called? Tick the correct option.

A Load ☐

B Fulcrum ☐

C Pivot point ☐

D Effort ☐

ICT Software

Applications of ICT

Computer software can perform many different functions from sorting data to drawing a design. There are many computer programs available for use, e.g. word processing packages, spreadsheets, desktop publishing packages and graphics packages.

Word Processing Packages

The most common package is Microsoft Word® and some of the most commonly used tools include…

- standard features such as **save**, **print**, **copy**, **paste**, etc.
- text formatting such as different text, font alignment, italics, etc.
- importing of graphics, e.g. **clip art**
- **mail merge** where letters can be personalised from a database.

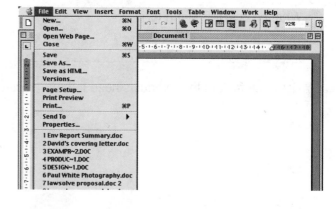

Spreadsheets

Spreadsheets are a program that enables information to be arranged onto a **grid** within a **range of cells**.

This allows the user to quickly assess the effect of varying one of the pieces of information on the project as a whole, e.g. cost.

It is also capable of interpreting the information as different types of graphs.

Spreadsheets can also do **mathematical calculations**. Formulae can be added so that the values in some cells can be automatically calculated, which is useful when making lists.

Anthropometric data

Sitting	Short	Average	Tall
Sitting height	795	880	965
Sitting eye height	685	765	845
Sitting elbow height	185	240	295
Popliteal height	355	420	490
Elbow-grip length	304	343	387
Buttock-popliteal length	435	488	550
Buttock-knee length	520	583	645

Hand size / grip	Small	Average	Large
Hand length	159	182	205
Palm length	89	102.5	116
Thumb length	40	49	58
Index finger length	60	69.5	79
Hand breadth	69	82	95
Maximum grip diameter	43	51	59

Desktop Publishing Packages

Desktop publishing packages are often used for designing magazines, newspapers and leaflets as this gives more control over the layout of a page.

A common package is Microsoft Publisher®. Pictures and text can be laid out on a page with images imported from other software and clip art libraries.

Graphics Packages

There are two main types of graphics:

- **Bitmap graphics** are made up of **pixels**, each of which contains specific colour information. The disadvantage of bitmap graphics is that they **lose detail** if they are scaled up, because the same number of pixels must be spread out over a larger area.
- **Vector graphics** consist of points, lines and curves which, when combined, can form complex objects. These objects can be filled with solid colours, gradients and even patterns. The advantage of vector graphics is that they can be scaled up with **no loss of detail** as the software works out the new co-ordinates to redraw the image.

Art packages are used for decorating graphic products, such as packaging. Examples include **CorelDRAW® Graphics Suite** and **Photoshop®**.

Drawing packages enable you to draw with lines and shapes. They now often contain a making program.

Computer Aided Design (CAD) is a sophisticated drawing package used by designers, engineers and architects to produce detailed drawings. CAD leads to the realisation of a product. Popular systems used in schools are ProDesktop® and **2D Design®**. In industry, the most popular system is AutoCAD®.

Painting Package

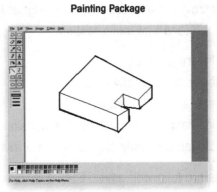

Drawing Package

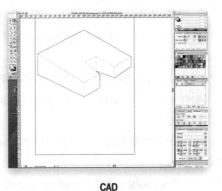

CAD

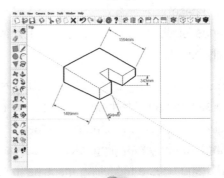

Quick Test

1. How do spreadsheets arrange their information?
2. What are art packages used for?
3. Name two popular CAD systems used in schools.
4. What Microsoft package can be used to produce magazines and newspapers?

KEY WORDS

Make sure you understand these words before moving on!

- Text formatting
- Spreadsheets
- Microsoft Publisher®
- Computer Aided Design (CAD)
- ProDesktop®
- AutoCAD®

CAD and CAM Systems

CAD Systems

CAD systems make it easier for a designer to produce an idea that **looks realistic.**

CAD software produces…
- orthographic 2D drawings
- 3D virtual reality models
- a wide range of symbols and dimensions, which can be easily placed onto a drawing.

CAD has the following **advantages** over drawing images by hand:
- CAD is much **quicker** and less time consuming.
- Objects can be drawn with **great accuracy** and scaled, rotated or reflected.
- Drawings can be **viewed from any angle**.
- It's **easier to make changes** at any stage of the drawing.
- CAD can **simulate how a product can perform** without using expensive testing methods.
- CAD can **store lots of information**, saving office space.
- Shapes, sizes, colours and surface textures can easily be altered.

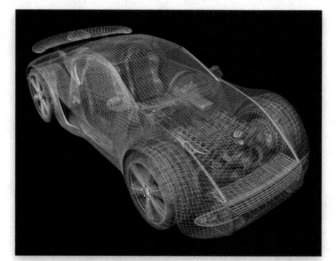

Like the system 'crating' by hand, the CAD system can use a 'wire frame' technique, where you can view right through an object (called **virtual modelling**). **Rapid prototyping** takes virtual designs from CAD and uses a modelling machine to see what the object will look like before final construction.

Computer Aided Manufacture

Computer Aided Manufacture (CAM) is used by engineers and machinists to make the product that has been designed.

Computers that control the manufacture of a product are **sent instructions via CAD** to make the components of that particular product.

CAM machines can work around the clock making objects.

CAD and CAM Systems

CAM Cutters

Signs can be made from vinyl using a **CAM cutter**. A CAM cutter works with a blade, plotting and cutting out from coordinates given by a computer.

When the shape is completely cut, the backing can be peeled off the **vinyl** and placed onto the sign's surface.

A CAM cutter can only cut shapes and not digital images.

Advantages of Using CAM

More and more manufacturing processes in industry are using computerised machines, for the following reasons:

- When programmed properly computers make less mistakes.
- Increased productivity and less human labour required as machines can carry on continuously.
- The standard of manufacture is very reliable and consistent.
- CAM can replace some of the jobs that are dangerous for people to do, e.g. by using **robots** in car manufacture.

Quick Test

1. CAD has many advantages. What is it quicker than?
2. What does CAM stand for?
3. What material are signs made from, which are fed through a CAM cutter?
4. What replaces humans when manufacture is dangerous?

KEY WORDS
Make sure you understand these words before moving on!
- Virtual reality
- Computer Aided Manufacture (CAM)
- CAM cutter
- Vinyl
- Robot

ICT Applications

The Internet

The World Wide Web (www) is the most common feature of the internet connecting you with websites and the email system.

It's a live form of communication which speeds up business and education throughout the world. The internet can be used to market and sell graphic products.

To connect to the internet you need...
- a computer
- a phone line
- a modem or ISDN connection
- an ISP (Internet Service Provider)
- browser software.

The internet includes the following functions:
- **www**: the World Wide Web stores millions of web pages on web servers.
- **HTML** (Hypertext Markup Language) is the language, or code, of web pages.
- **Website**: this is a set of web pages created by a person or an organisation.
- **Surfing**: moving around the internet by using a program which enables you to read the pages at different sites, e.g. Netscape or Internet Explorer.
- **Search Engine**: used to search the net for a particular topic, possibly using Yahoo, Excite, Lycos, Google, etc.
- **Email** (electronic mail): worldwide communication.

Computer Input Devices

Computer **input** devices allow data to be entered into a computer.

Bar codes are vertical bars in different groups read by an optical scanner. They contain product information, e.g. stock control data, origin and product identity. Bar codes are printed on almost everything you buy, as they are durable and cheap to produce.

A **graphics tablet** is a flat pad, where the designer uses a special pen to create an accurate image on the screen.

A **concept keyboard** is a grid of buttons on a flat board, which contains information and a description or picture on each button. They are used commonly on fast food tills.

A **scanner** is a cheap way of transferring images onto the computer.

A **digital camera** stores a digital photographic image, which is read by a computer.

Other input devices include **CD ROM**, **memory sticks** and **memory cards**.

Bar Code

Graphics Tablet

Scanner

Digital Camera

Computer Output Devices

Computer **output** devices are used to take information out of a computer.

The following devices allow information to be downloaded to the user in the form of a 'hard' copy:

- **Ink-jet printers** are generally cheap to buy although quality and speed levels are a drawback.
- **Laser printers** produce very high-quality prints. They are more expensive than ink-jet printers.
- **Plotters** are used for A3, or bigger sized drawings. They are used mainly in conjunction with CAD and CAM applications. Output is accurate and of very high quality.

Ink-jet Printer

Digital Media and New Technology

Companies today are able to enhance their business trade by using digital media and new technology, such as graphics, photos, image libraries and multimedia presentations. Here are some other examples:

- **Programmable IC's** – programmable devices, e.g. digital timers on thermostats.
- **Audio Visual** – information that's presented in sound (audio) and image (visual) format rather than in text format, e.g. VHS tapes, CDs, etc.
- **Bluetooth®** – uses radio technology to exchange data over short distances from mobile devices.
- **High-definition television (HDTV)** – a digital system, which broadcasts higher resolution pictures than traditional TV.
- **Radiofrequency identification tags (RFID)** – an identification method, which stores and remotely receives data from identification tags. They can be put on products, animals and passports.
- **Electronic Point of Sale (EPOS)** – chip and pin systems, which help to process the most popular products from the warehouse to the point of sale in the shortest time possible.
- **Commercial digital printing** – capable of short print runs and large format prints.

Quick Test

1. Name three output devices.
2. What does www stand for?
3. What sizes of paper does a plotter print drawings at?
4. Fill in the missing word:
5. A _____ is a cheap way of transferring images onto a computer.

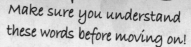

KEY WORDS

Make sure you understand these words before moving on!

- ISDN
- HTML
- Input
- Output

Safety Hazards and Control

Safety Hazards

It's important that you develop an awareness for dangerous / hazardous situations in your working environment. Some of the machines and tools you use can cause an injury if you don't follow safe procedures.

In a workshop, machine guards and dust and fume extractors are installed for a safe environment. You must always wear safety / protective equipment when working on machinery.

When you're designing a product, you have to take into consideration any safety hazards for the user, e.g. sharp edges on toys could cause harm.

Standards

The Health and Safety Executive (HSE) is responsible for making sure all schools and working environments are safe to work in. **Risk assessments** are carried out so appropriate measures can be taken. The HSE have the power to close a place down if the place is in breach of its health and safety regulations.

The **BSI** have devised tests to check that products are **safe and reliable**. They award the **Kitemark** to show that the product meets the relevant standards.

HSE Literature

Kitemark

Asbestos kills: Protect yourself!
You are more at risk than you think

Safety Symbols

You need to be able to understand safety symbols in the workshop to avoid accidents happening:
- **Red** signs tell you that you 'cannot' do something because it may be very **dangerous**.
- **Blue** signs are **mandatory** and tell you that a particular action must be undertaken.
- **Green** signs are **safety signs**.
- **Yellow** signs show a **warning**.
- **Orange** signs show toxic **chemical warnings**.

No smoking

Foot protection must be worn

First aid post

CAUTION ATTENTION
WET FLOOR PLANCHER MOUILLE

2WB
2447
CORROSIVE
SPECIALIST ADVICE

Quality Control

Quality control is a **series of checks** that are carried out on a product as it's made. The checks make sure that each product meets a **specific standard**. Some likely tests to be carried out on the product include checking…

* **size**
* **weight**
* **colour**
* **form**.

Testing is an important part of the manufacture of a product. It can take place anytime during production, e.g. an injection-moulded bottle top could be tested after ten, a thousand or a million have been produced. Some of the tests would include checking its diameter, thickness and whether it screws properly onto its container.

As every object can't be guaranteed to accurately meet the specifications when produced in large quantities, a **tolerance** has to be applied. This specifies the allowed **minimum** and **maximum measurements**.

Analysis of tolerance tests can signal the imminent failure of a machine and can help to achieve the ultimate aim of quality control which is **zero faults**.

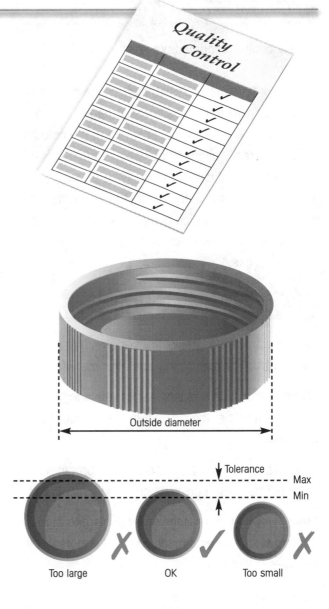

Outside diameter

Tolerance

Max
Min

Too large   OK   Too small

Quick Test

1. What range of measurements does a tolerance test do on a product?
2. Name four things that are considered when checking the quality of a product.
3. What is the ultimate aim you need to achieve when you do a quality control?
4. What does an orange sign mean in a workshop?
5. What is the HSE responsible for?

KEY WORDS
Make sure you understand these words before moving on!
* Hazards
* HSE
* BSI
* Quality control
* Tolerance
* Zero faults

Safety Hazards and Control

Quality Control of Printed Products

Quality control in printed products is aided by the use of…

- **colour bars** that are used to check the consistency and density of colours on each page
- **registration marks** that ensure that the colours are correctly aligned (they should appear black when viewed using a magnifying glass)
- **crop marks** to cut the product to the correct size
- **visual checks** which ensure that there are no breaks in the typeface and all text is clear and legible.

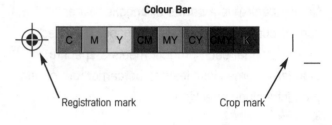

Colour Bar

| C | M | Y | CM | MY | CY | CMY | K |

Registration mark   Crop mark

Quality Assurance

Quality assurance checks the systems that make the products, before, during and after manufacture.

Quality assurance ensures that **consistency** is achieved and that the product is of the **required standard**.

Factors such as equipment, materials, processes and staff training need to be constantly monitored.

Make sure that you recognise symbols and signs relating to quality assurance, that are endorsed by recognised authorities.

Non-Destructive / Destructive Testing

There are two types of quality assurance tests carried out.

Non-destructive tests are carried out to ensure that the product works, **without causing any damage** to the product. For example, doing visual tests.

In a **destructive test**, a sample of products are made to be tested for their strength; they will be **tested until they are damaged** or completely broken.

Questions for Quality Assurance

To ensure a high level of quality the following questions can be asked to assess any product (including your own):

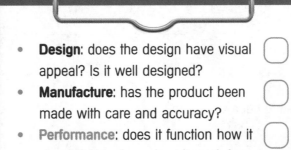

- **Design**: does the design have visual appeal? Is it well designed?
- **Manufacture**: has the product been made with care and accuracy?
- **Performance**: does it function how it should? How long does it work for without breaking down?
- **Customer views**: is the customer happy with the product? Do they think it works well? Is it cheap enough or value for money?
- **Overall views**: what do you think of your own design? Does it meet the original specification?

Quick Test

1. Colour bars are checking for what on printed products?
2. What are the two quality assurance tests carried out on products?
3. What four factors need to be constantly checked for quality assurance?
4. What is a destructive test aiming to do?
5. Give two examples of questions that could be asked to assess the quality of any product.

KEY WORDS

Make sure you understand these words before moving on!
- Colour bars
- Registration marks
- Crop marks
- Visual checks
- Quality assurance
- Performance

Practice Questions

1. Name four different advantages of using CAD against hand-drawn designs.

   a) .... b) ....

   c) .... d) ....

2. Explain how CAD and CAM work together.

   ....

   ....

3. What machine would be used to cut a vinyl sign?

   ....

4. What is the World Wide Web also known as?

   ....

5. Which of the following are computer output devices? Tick the correct options.

   A Inkjet printer ◯   **B** Bar code ◯

   C Scanner ◯   **D** Plotter ◯

   E Laser printer ◯   **F** Digital camera ◯

6. Name five computer input devices.

   a) .... b) ....

   c) .... d) ....

   e) ....

7. What is a plotter?

   ....

8. Give an example of a command that you would find on a red safety symbol.

   ....

9 What is quality control?

_____

_____

10 Explain what a tolerance is when doing a quality control check.

_____

11 On a printed product, what is a registration mark for?

_____

12 What is a non-destructive test?

_____

_____

13 What is quality assurance?

_____

_____

14 Give examples of three tools most commonly used in word processing packages.

a) _____

b) _____

c) _____

15 Which of the following equipment are required for connection to the internet? Tick the correct options.

A Scanner ☐

B Phone line ☐

C Plotter ☐

D Modem ☐

E An ISP ☐

Useful Symbols

Packaging Symbols

 **Keep Britain Tidy** – Aimed at making people aware that they have a responsibility to keep the environment tidy and litter free.

 **Fair Trade Symbol** – Occasionally seen on packaging. This symbol guarantees that the farmers and workers in lesser developed (LED) countries receive a fair price for their goods.

 **Conformité Europeene 'CE' Symbol** – Tells you that the product meets the minimum requirements from the EU directive to be allowed to be put on sale.

 **Eco-label** – Awarded to businesses that are producing products, which are kind to the environment.

 **Fragile**

 **Keep Dry**

This Side Up

Recycling Symbols

 **Mobius Loop** – Guarantees that the packaging is recyclable.

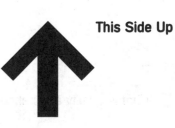 **Mobius Loop with Percentage** – If the centre of the mobius loop contains a number, the item is made from that percentage of recycled materials.

 **'Green Dot' Symbol** – Used on packaging in many European countries to signify that the producer has made a contribution towards the recycling of packaging.

 **Recyclable Aluminium** – Drinks cans may have this symbol, showing that the material can be recycled.

 **Recyclable Steel** – The object can be placed in a steel recycling facility.

 **Glass** – This symbol reminds consumers to recycle bottles and glass jars at bottle banks or through kerbside collection schemes.

Plastics

These symbols identify the type of plastic:

Polyethylene Terepthalate – Fizzy drink bottles and oven-ready meal trays.

High Density Polyethylene – Bottles for milk and washing up liquids.

Polyvinyl Chloride (PVC) – Food trays, cling film, bottles for squash, mineral water and shampoo.

Low Density Polyethylene – Carrier bags and bin liners.

Polypropylene – Margarine tubs, microwaveable meal trays.

Polystyrene – Yoghurt pots, foam meat or fish trays, hamburger boxes and egg cartons, vending cups, plastic cutlery, protective packaging for electronic goods and toys.

Other – Any other plastics that do not fall into any of the above categories, e.g. melamine which is often used in plastic plates and cups.

Glossary

Alignment of text – where the text is positioned within a column.

Anthropometrics – data relating to measurements of the human body.

Architect – a designer who designs buildings.

Batch production – a limited number of products being produced at any one time.

Biodegradable – organic substances which are broken down naturally over a period of time.

Blow moulding – air is blown into a mould, to force plastic to the sides of a mould; to create a hollow product.

Brand name – name of a product a company has produced.

Carbon fibre – a very strong, light, carbonized acrylic thread, which is used to reinforce resins, metals, and ceramics, making turbine blades.

Clic rivets – two plastics rivets which hold two sheets of material together and 'clic' into place.

Colour separation – a method of separating out the four process colours, prior to printing.

Comb binding – a method used to bind pages together into a book. This method uses round plastic spines with rings, which go through rectangular holes.

Complementary colours – opposite colours on the colour wheel, which go well together.

Compression moulding – a hydraulic press applies a downward force to create a shape from material.

Construction lines – fine drawing lines which help to work as a grid on a drawing.

Contrast – when one colour stands out against another, e.g. light against dark.

Copyright – the legal right of companies to control the use and reproduction of their original works.

Corporate identity – commercial logo which represents what the company is all about.

Corrugation – two flat layers of outer material and an inner fluted material.

COSHH – Control Of Substances Hazardous to Health.

Crash lock – a net of a box, which is folded and assembled by the base folding out and locking into an open position.

Crating – construction lines forming a box to help sketch a 3D object.

Creasing bar – a metal bar on a machine which creates a fold in the material (mostly card).

Cultures – society, traditions and customs of people.

Die cutter – metal cutter, like a pastry cutter, that cuts the outline of a shape, e.g. net of a box.

Dimensioning – a measurement of something in one or more directions such as length, width, or height.

Disassembly – analysing each part of a product.

Eco-footprint – a measure of the human demand on the Earth's natural resources.

Elevation – a plan, side or front view on a drawing.

Ellipse – a shape representing an oval.

Embossing – raises or indents selected areas of a design.

Emulsion – a water-based paint that usually has a matt finish.

Encapsulation – to enclose something completely in two layers of plastic film.

Environment – our surroundings; all the external factors influencing the life and activities of people, plants, and animals.

EPOS (Electronic Point of Sale) – a computer system that scans bar codes.

Ergonomics – application of scientific information to the design of objects, systems and the environment, for human use.

Exhibition designer – designs displays for a company to promote their products.

Exploded view – a drawing showing separate parts of an object.

Extrusion – where plastics are pushed through a mould to create 'rod-like' shapes.

Eyelets – a small ring of metal fixed to a hole.

Flow chart – a series of tasks shown in different action boxes to help plan your work.

Font – printed or screen characters of the same design and size.

French curve – designed to help draw curves.

Function – the need and use of a product.

Fusion – where dots of colour blend together to appear another colour.

Gantt chart – a chart which helps you to plan the tasks and deadline dates.

Gears – a toothed mechanical part, e.g. a wheel that engages with a similar toothed part to transmit motion from one rotating body to another.

Graphite – lead in pencils.

Hexagon – a two-dimensional geometric shape with six sides.

High Density Polyethylene (HDPE) – a plastic used for buckets, pipes and bowls.

Holographic – layers of metallic foil, showing a 3D pattern effect.

Horizon line – place where the sky meets the ground in the distance.

Hue – the tone / shade of a colour.

Hydroelectric dam – the generation of electricity by means of water pressure into a dam.

Ideogram – a symbol or graphical character used to represent an idea or thing, e.g. @ or &.

Injection moulding – manufacturing process where plastics are injected into a mould to make a shape.

Isometric projection – 30°-angled, scaled 3D drawing.

Jig – holds the object / material in place to be worked on for bending to shape, cutting or drilling.

Justified text – where the text and images align along both the left and right hand margins.

Kerning – where the spacing of letters is adjusted in pairs to make them more evenly spaced.

Kinetic energy – an energy produced by a motion, such as wind.

Kitemark – symbol of trust, integrity and quality.

Lamination – bonding together thin layers of materials to form a composite material.

Laser cutting – where material is cut on a machine, using a laser beam.

Linear – a movement in one direction.

Line bending – to heat and bend plastic in one straight line.

Lithography – a four colour printing process.

Logo – a symbol, sign or emblem which helps to promote a company.

Low Density Polyethylene (LDPE) – a plastic used for carrier bags, packaging and film.

Lubricant – sulphides and waxes added to plastic to make the polymer easier to form.

Mass production – products produced on mass and sometimes in continuous manufacture.

Medium Density Fibre Board (MDF) – a manufactured fibreboard, with no grain.

Microencapsulation – microscopic bubbles capture tiny particles of scent. When the surface is scratched these particles are released.

Non-biodegradable – items which can't be decomposed or mineralised by microorganisms.

Non-renewable energy – energy resources which can't be replaced in a lifetime.

Octagon – a two-dimensional geometric shape with eight sides and eight angles.

Glossary

Oscillating – a movement which is swinging in alternate directions.

Paper fasteners – a metal component used to thread through a hole and hold two pieces of paper or card together.

Parallelogram – a two-dimensional geometric shape with four sides, in which both pairs of opposite sides are parallel and of equal length, and the opposite angles are equal.

Pastels – 'chalk' like crayons, which can be used to colour sketches.

Patent – an official document that grants a right to a company to make a product that no one can copy.

Pentagon – a two-dimensional shape with five sides and five angles.

Perspective – realistic drawing in 3D of an object with vanishing points.

Phosphorescent – a 'glow in the dark' fluorescent material.

Photochromic – a material that changes colour in response to light intensity.

Piezoelectric – when voltage is applied to a material it changes shape.

Pigments – added colour to plastic.

Pivot point (fulcrum) – the point about which something can rotate.

Planometric – a 3D drawing which uses 45° angles.

Plasticisers – a substance added to plastic to make it less brittle.

Polyester resin (PR) – a resin and hardener which are mixed together and laminated onto car bodies and boats.

Polygon – a two-dimensional geometric shape with three or more straight sides.

Polymerisation – when monomers join together to form a long chain of molecules called polymers.

Polypropylene (PP) – commonly used plastic for food containers, storage and household products.

Polystyrene (PS) – a low density plastic used for absorbing shock in packaging.

Polyvinyl acetate (PVA) – a white adhesive used for gluing wood or card.

Polyvinyl chloride (PVC) – plastics used for bottles and blister packs.

Pressfit – relies on tensile and compression for two parts to stay together.

Primary colours – colours which can't be made from another colour.

ProDesktop – 3D software package.

Propelling pencil – mechanical lead pencil.

Proportion – relationship of size.

Prototype – model made to test, find faults and amend before production starts.

Protractor – used to measure angles.

Pulley – a wheel with a grooved rim over which a belt can move to change the direction of a moving force.

Quadrilateral – a two-dimensional geometric shape with four sides.

Rapid prototyping – a computer-based drawing that can check the validity of a potential product.

Ratio – mathematical term for scale.

Reciprocal – a backwards and forwards movement.

Recyclable – to dispose of an object in view to it being reused in some form or another.

Registered – when a company legally records the ownership of their products.

Rendering – using tone and colour to create a realistic drawing of a product.

Renewable energy – will not run out.

Rhombus – a parallelogram that has four equal sides and oblique angles.

Sans serif – letters without the extra strokes on the end of the stems.

Scale ruler – a ruler which has scales already worked out.

Schematic map – a map which shows directions using graphic symbols.

Secondary colours – produced by mixing two primary colours together.

Serif – lettering strokes, which finish off the end of a stem on a letter.

Set square – helps you to draw set angles on your drawings.

Shape memory alloy (SMA) – metal alloys which remember the original shape.

Smart materials – materials which can respond to changes in their environment.

Solar – using the Sun's radiation as a source of energy.

Spacing – the ease in which text can be read according to the space between the letters.

Specification – a detailed description, which provides information needed to make, build or produce something.

Stabiliser – an additive to plastic to prevent moisture or UV light affecting the surface.

Styrofoam™ – a trademark for a light plastics / foam type material used in modelling or packaging.

Sustainability – meeting human needs without depleting natural resources.

Target market – who the product is being designed for.

Texture – surface pattern or decoration.

Thermochromic – materials that respond to changes in temperature by changing colour.

Thermoplastics – plastics which can be reheated and remoulded.

Thermosetting plastics – plastics which can't be reheated and moulded.

Three dimensions (3D) – the ability to see three sides of an object at any one time.

Tolerances – allowance made for something to deviate within a set range of minimum and maximum sizes.

Tone – light and dark shadows on an object.

Tracking – increasing or decreasing the space between all letters in a block of text to make it more evenly spaced.

Trademark – a brand name or a symbol which represents the service a company gives.

Transparent – see through material.

Trapezium – quadrilateral with two parallel sides.

Tuck in – a tab on a box, which is used to help hold the lid shut.

Typesetting – the process of arranging text for printing, by using computers or arranging blocks of type manually.

Typography – the art / style of lettering.

Urea formaldehyde – hard brittle plastic, used for domestic appliances and electrics.

UV varnishing – high gloss finish applied to a printed area.

Vacuum forming - a sheet of plastic is heated and stretched onto a mould. A vacuum is applied to remove air, to shape the plastic.

Velcro™ – brand name for hook and loop fasteners.

Virtual reality – computer simulates a three-dimensional physical environment using visual stimuli where somebody can see an object in reality.

Working drawing – 2D scaled drawing, for manufacture of a product.

Workplanes – surfaces you are working on in ProDesktop.

Answers

QUICK TEST ANSWERS

Page 5
1. Crating
2. Areas of light and shadow
3. Blue and red
4. Opposite each other
5. Add some black paint

Page 7
1. Peace and keeps the bad spirits away
2. **Any two of the following:** Growth; Renewal; Environment; Envy; Balance; Harmony
3. Colours could be offensive according to someone's faith.
4. Logos are symbols that convey a meaning.
5. A word, phrase, symbol or design which identifies and distinguishes the goods of one company
6. A logo or title which represents what a company is all about

Page 9
1. Serifs are letters which have strokes on the end of the stems.
2. Sans serifs are letters without the extra strokes on the ends.
3. **Any four suitable answers, for example:** Full bracketed; Hairline; Slab; Slab bracketed
4. Upper case letters
5. The art of lettering
6. The alignment of text within a column where the text sits flush with the left and right hand margins

Page 11
1. For packing objects
2. Thin, fairly transparent white paper
3. Cartridge paper
4. Over 200g/m^2
5. Millimetres, centimetres and inches (or mm, cm and inches)

ANSWERS TO PRACTICE QUESTIONS

Pages 12–13
1. Square grid
2.
3. **a)–b) In any order:** To become a well-recognised company name; To be identified with well-known brands of products
4. It means it is a registered company.
5. Adjusting the spacing of two letters that are beside each other
6. **a) In any order:** Red; Blue; Yellow
   b) Primary colours
7. Complementary colours
8. Healthy and organic products / Environmental
9. To help you get the angles correct in isometric projection
10. **a)–c) Any suitable answers, for example:** Changing the size; Using italic; Using a different typeface
11. Where dots of colour blend together to create another colour, e.g. a mixture of red and blue dots will appear purple.
12. Strokes or serifs
13. To make the words easier to read.
14. **a)** False **b)** True **c)** False

QUICK TEST ANSWERS

Page 15
1. Measures angles
2. Different scales that have already been worked out
3. **Any from:** Graphite pencils; coloured pencils
4. Covering larger areas with colour
5. False

Page 17
1. **In any order:** 1:20, 1:25, 1:50, 1:100
2. 1:2
3. Above
4. 45 / 45 degrees or 60 / 30 degrees
5. A parallelogram has four sides and is a quadrilateral shape.

Page 21
1. A 3D object to scale
2. Shows how an object fits together.
3. Eye line
4. False
5. British Standards Institution

Page 23
1. Above and in the middle
2. To protect a new design / idea and stop others from making, using, importing or selling the invention without your permission
3. Using Computer Aided Design (CAD)
4. **In any order:** Plan; Front elevation; Two side elevations

ANSWERS TO PRACTICE QUESTIONS

Pages 24–25
1. Ellipse template
2. Isometric projection
3. Draw curves / arcs
4. 'Push' mechanism
5. B
6. Fineline
7. **a)–b) In any order:** Fine line technical pen; Fibre tipped pen
8. Working drawings / Orthographic projection
9. Top left or top middle of the drawing
10. Planometric – 45 / 45 degrees
    Perspective – Two point
    Crating – no measured angle
    Isometric – 30 degrees
11. 2:1
12. **a)–c) Any three suitable answers, for example:** Overhead projector; Photocopier; Computer software
13. 6
14. **Any suitable answers, for example:** You can see all the components clearly; It is to scale; All parts are in relative positions to each other – as if blown apart by an explosion.
15. Horizon line
16. Interiors
17. Quality, trust and integrity
18. BSI (British Standards Institution)

Answers

Design & Market Influences

Page 27
1. The underground map
2. 1921
3. Road signs / the signage system
4. Corporate identity and branding
5. Pop-up books

Page 29
1. **Any three suitable answers, for example:** Weight; Smell; Shape; Light; Noise; Size; Temperature; Legibility of writing; Style and colour of font; Colour contrast
2. One colour can stand out from another
3. Data that is supplied by the British Standards Institution based on the sizes of people
4. The local library
5. Millimetres

Page 33
1. Hands
2. Target market
3. **Any suitable answers, for example:** Glass; Paper
4. Sustainability is about meeting the needs and wants of society without depleting resources.

Page 35
1. False
2. Non-biodegradable products are often synthetic and can't be broken down naturally.
3. Landfill sites
4. Kinetic energy is energy produced by a motion such a wind.

ANSWERS TO PRACTICE QUESTIONS
Pages 36–37
1. **a)–b) Any two from:** Buy reusable products; Reuse items; Donate to charity, Re-sell items
2. **a)–f) In any order:** Reduce; Reuse; Recycle; Refuse; Repair; Rethink
3. Landfill sites are where local authorities and industry take waste to be buried and compacted with other wastes under the ground.
4. a) Biodegradable means that materials are organic substances which are broken down naturally over a period of time.
   b) **Any suitable answer, for example:** Newspapers, Magazines, Card packaging
5. Heat energy from the Sun
6. **a)–c) Any three suitable answers, for example:** Wind turbines; Solar energy; Biofuel
7. An ecological footprint is a measure of human demand on the Earth's natural resources and the Earth's ability to keep up with the demands humans put on it.
8. The Environment Agency
9. Carbon footprint is a measure of the impact of human activities on the environment in terms of the amount of carbon dioxide produced.
10. The Underground map (schematic map)
11. a) Famous artists and designers
    b) i)–ii) **Any suitable answers, for example:** Salvador Dali; Michael Graves
12. B and C
13. A schematic map represents the elements of a system using graphic symbols.
14. False
15. Who is likely to buy the product
16. The process of a product becoming obsolete or breaking down after a period of use.
17. Looking at a product, taking it apart and working out how it was made

Materials & Processes

QUICK TEST ANSWERS
Page 39
1. A fluted centre
2. Resin W™ or Unibond™
3. **Any one from:** Difficult to cut, form and join together; Brittle
4. Expensive to buy
5. **In any order:** Sticking pieces of paper together; Used as a photo mount
6. Spray Mount

Page 41
1. Pastry cutters
2. Circles
3. Scoring with a knife
4. Lamination
5. Shiny finish

Page 43
1. **In any order:** Water soluble; Water resistant; Solvent based
2. Tensile and compression
3. To reinforce holes in material
4. Mechanical movement

Page 45
1. Precious metal clays
2. Temperature
3. Light intensity
4. **Any suitable answers, for example:** racing cars; aircraft, bicycles
5. Phosphorescent

Page 49
1. Thermoplastics
2. Plastic granules / powder
3. Air is blown into the mould
4. Thermosetting plastics

Page 51
1. Thermoplastics
2. Air
3. Mirrors
4. Helps to bend or shape materials to the right shape or angle
5. Acrylic

Page 53
1. **Any suitable answer, for example:** An exhibition stand
2. **Any suitable answer, for example:** Milk carton
3. **In any order:** Letterpressing; Block printing
4. The metal letters have to be individually made
5. Flexography uses flexible rubber or plastic plates for cylinders instead of flat printing plates.

Page 55
1. Photographically
2. Dots
3. A rubber-bladed squeegee
4. Stencils
5. Cyan, magenta, yellow, black

Answers

ANSWERS TO PRACTICE QUESTIONS
Pages 58–59
1. D
2. Using a line bending machine and a bending jig
3. Motor actuators
4. **a)–c) In any order:** Phenol; Urea formaldehyde; Melamine formaldehyde
5. Liquid crystals or metal compounds
6. **a)** Afterglow or glow in the dark materials
   b) By paint or spray
7. Compression moulding
8. **a)–c) In any order:** Wear a safety mask; Dispose of rags after use; Wear gloves/barrier cream to protect your hands
9. **a)** Grommets
   b) Two parts
   c) Using die cutters
10. Transparent tape which is self adhesive on both sides of the tape
11. Protects your fingers from being cut
12. Peel it off after you have painted or used pastels
13. Coping saw
14. Embossing

Packaging & Mechanisms

QUICK TEST ANSWERS
Page 61
1. **In any order:** Preserve; Protect; Promote; Transport
2. Net
3. Crash lock
4. Tessellation
5. Crates or cartons

Page 63
1. Paper bags or labels
2. Fluting
3. High Density Polyethylene
4. **Any one from:** Detergent bottles; Milk and fruit juice bottles; Bottle caps; frozen food packaging
5. Foil lamination

Page 65
1. Plastic bottles are safer than glass – breakages in the bathroom would be dangerous.
2. **In any order:** Rotating; Linear; Reciprocating; Oscillating
3. Fulcrum
4. It's expensive and can shatter
5. **Any two suitable answers, for example:** It is waterproof; Transparent; Readily available, Recyclable, Reusable.

Page 67
1. Second class lever
2. Bicep
3. Linear
4. Up and down

Page 69
1. **In any order:** Extension; Compression; Radial movement; Twisting
2. motion
3. **In any order:** To control how fast something turns; To make lifting things easier
4. Makes the wheels turn in the opposite direction
5. In 3D working models/display models.

Page 71
1. Blunt knife and metal safety ruler
2. 90 degrees
3. Rotary mechanism
4. In the centre

ANSWERS TO PRACTICE QUESTIONS
Pages 72–73
1. Point of Sale
2. **a)** Incised mechanism **b)** Layer mechanism
   c) Sliding mechanism
3. **a)–b) In any order:** Hold a metal ruler against the fold; Use a creasing bar
4. A net is a two dimensional shape which when scored, folded and glued together forms a three-dimensional package.
5. **a)** To press out the shape of the development
   b) A fold
6. **a)** Net **b)** Waste material
7. The tab on the end of a lid, which holds the lid closed
8. Bottles
9. Corrugated cardboard
10. Low density polyethylene
11. **a)–c) In any order:** Light; Oxygen; Moisture
12. **a)** How fast something turns
    b) **Any suitable answer, for example:** In cassette recorders; In washing machines.
13. Gears are used as force multipliers or reducers to make things go faster or slower.
14. Reciprocating
15. D

Information & Communication Technology

QUICK TEST ANSWERS

Page 75
1. On grids
2. Decorating graphic products
3. ProDesktop® and 2D Design®
4. Microsoft Publisher®

Page 77
1. Drawing images by hand
2. Computer Aided Manufacture
3. Vinyl sheet
4. Robots

Page 79
1. **Any three suitable answers, for example:** Ink-jet printers; Laser printers; Plotters
2. World Wide Web
3. A3 or bigger
4. scanner

Page 81
1. Minimum and maximum
2. **In any order:** Size; Weight; Colour; Form
3. Zero faults
4. Chemical warning
5. Making sure all schools and working environments are safe to work in.

Page 83
1. Consistency and density of colour
2. Destructive and non-destructive
3. **In any order:** Equipment, materials, processes, staff training
4. Test for the strength of a product
5. **Any two suitable answers, for example:** Does the product function as it should? Is the customer happy with the product?

ANSWERS TO PRACTICE QUESTIONS

Pages 84–85
1. **a)–d) Any four suitable answers, for example:** Can easily change things; Quicker and less time consuming than drawing by hand; You can view right through an object; CAD can send messages to CAM to make a product
2. Computers which run the manufacture of products are sent information via CAD to make components of a product.
3. **Any from:** CAMM1; CAM; 2D CAMM
4. www. / Net
5. A, D, E
6. **a)–e) Any five suitable answers, for example:** Concept keyboard; Graphics tablet; Scanner; Digital camera; Bar code; CD ROM; Memory stick; Memory card
7. A large (A3 or above) printer using pens to draw lines and lettering
8. **Any suitable answer, for example:** Stop sign; No entry
9. A series of checks that are carried out on a product as it's made to make sure that the product meets a specific standard
10. When you check the minimum and maximum size of a product
11. To ensure that the colours are correctly aligned
12. Non-destructive tests are carried out to ensure that the product works, without causing any damage, e.g. doing visual tests.
13. Quality assurance checks the systems that make the products, before, during and after manufacture.
14. **a)–c) Any three suitable answers, for example:** Save; Print; Copy; Paste; Text formatting; Importing graphics; Mail merge.
15. B, D and E

Index

Acknowledgements

p.4 ©iStockphoto.com/Royce DeGrie
p.7 ©Cadbury
p.7 Reproduced by kind permission of Royal Mail Group Ltd. All rights reserved.
p.10 ©iStockphoto.com/ Slawomir Jastrzebski
p.14 ©iStockphoto.com/ Matthew Rambo
p.14 ©iStockphoto.com
p.14 ©iStockphoto.com/Alan Goulet
p.15 ©iStockphoto.com/Yiap See Fat
p.15 ©iStockphoto.com
p.21 ©Kevin White
p.22 Kitemark reproduced with kind permission of BSI Product Services, www.kitemark.com.
p.23 ©Hamish Sanderson
p.26 ©London Transport Museum
p.26 'Anna G' corkscrew designed by Alessandro Mendini 1994. Alessi Spa, Crusinallo, Italy.

p.26 'Juicy Salif' lemon squeezer designed by Philippe Starck 1990. Alessi Spa, Crusinallo, Italy.
p.27 ©iStockphoto.com/Jeff Dalton
p.27 Reproduced by kind permission of Prudential plc
p.27 Courtesy of www.robertsabuda.com
p.30 ©iStockphoto.com/Kevin Thomas
p.30 ©iStockphoto.com/Tracy Hebden
p.30 ©iStockphoto.com/Tomas Bercic
p.30 ©iStockphoto.com/ Nicholas Monu
p.31 ©iStockphoto.com
p.31 ©iStockphoto.com/Susan Trigg
p.42 ©iStockphoto.com/Alex Potemkin
p.43 ©iStockphoto.com/Craig Veltri
p.51 ©iStockphoto.com/ Paul Mckeown
p.51 ©iStockphoto.com/Chris Fertnig
p.53 ©iStockphoto.com/ Matthew Dixon
p.53 ©iStockphoto.com

p.54 ©iStockphoto.com/Gregor Inkret
p.56 ©iStockphoto.com/Bonita Hein
p.56 ©iStockphoto.com
p.63 ©iStockphoto.com/ Dawn Liljenquist
p.63 ©iStockphoto.com/Eliza Snow
p.63 ©iStockphoto.com/Rafa Irusta
p.63 ©iStockphoto.com
p.63 ©iStockphoto.com/Travis Manley
p.74 ©DEFRA
p.74 ©The National Coal Mining Museum for England
p.76 ©iStockphoto.com/Mark Evans
p.76 ©iStockphoto.com/ Ricardo Azoury
p.80 Reproduced with kind permission of HSE. For further information, please visit www.hse.gov.uk
p.80 Kitemark reproduced with kind permission of BSI Product Services, www.kitemark.com.
p.83 ©iStockphoto.com/Julien Grondin

The following images are reproduced with the kind permission of Rapid Electronics Ltd., Severalls Lane, Colchester, Essex CO4 5JS. www.rapidonline.com
p.14 342504
p.14 342500
p.14 342050
p.15 067750
p.40 858330
p.42 343702
p.43 871872
p.62 452034

Controlled Assessment Guide
p.5 ©iStockphoto.com/Julien Grondin
p.13 ©iStockphoto.com/Ben Greer

All other images ©2009 Jupiterimages Corporation, and Letts and Lonsdale.